CREATORS
NOT CONSUMERS

THE **GRAVITY PAYMENTS** CULTURE BOOK

ACKNOWLEDGMENTS

Although there is only one writer named, there are many people who helped make this book possible. Emery Wager first proposed the idea and set the original vision. James Pratt embraced that vision and shepherded the project to completion. Bobby Powers provided valuable feedback on countless rounds and revisions. Tammi Kroll helped me figure out the best way to talk about our management philosophy. Dan Price shared his views on culture and many of the values discussed in the book. Nelson Pfab and Oliver Heneghan offered guidance on inclusive language. Stefan Bennett, Aaron Hart, and Korinne Ward gave suggestions based on their unique experiences and perspectives at the company. Marta Anthony, Alex Franklin, Jena Miller, Ian Nisbet, and Chloe Vega explained and clarified company policies and procedures to ensure the book was accurate. Jeremy Salvo designed the cover and layout in record time, despite the fact that I gave him the manuscript a week later than he asked for it. Jess Dho reminded me of the value of deadlines.

The stories presented in this book were gathered at an all-company meeting in 2018 as well as through my own observations and discussions with team members. I interviewed dozens of people about the stories they felt best embodied Gravity's values and worked with them to make sure those stories were presented as accurately as possible. This book would be dreadfully dull without their contributions.

Most of all, thank you to each and every person at Gravity for creating a culture worth writing about.

Brooke Carey
Lead Storyteller
August 2019

TABLE OF CONTENTS

Introduction: Our Mission and Culture   1

Part 1: Creative Leadership   11
    Chapter 1: Be Your Own CEO   14
    Chapter 2: Transparency   25
    Chapter 3: Customer-Centric Hierarchy   30

Part II: Passion for Progress   39
    Chapter 4: A Culture of Candor   42
    Chapter 5: We Hire People, Not Resumes   53
    Chapter 6: Diversity and Inclusion   66

Part III: Responsibility   73
    Chapter 7: Integrity   76
    Chapter 8: Empathy   84
    Chapter 9: Teamwork   92

Part IV: Our Compensation Philosophy   97

In Closing   104

Appendix A   105

INTRODUCTION
OUR MISSION AND CULTURE

"We exist to stand with the little gal or guy who believes in the American Dream and is willing to work to chase it."

This is the guiding philosophy and mission statement at Gravity, but it's not just a nice catchphrase we decided to paint on our wall. Nor is it merely a tagline we use in our PR and marketing materials or a platitude designed to help in the recruiting process. It is, in fact, the lifeblood of our company, the reason we exist, and the principle behind what we do every day.

Although you *will* see this phrase on our walls and in our marketing and recruiting materials, this philosophy lives outside of these static places and is communicated throughout the company on a daily basis. You'll hear it in conversations we have with each other, with our merchants, and with anyone who asks, "So, what do you do here anyway?" It is a statement that informs every decision we make and action we take, whether at an individual or company-wide level.

When we speak about the little guy or gal, we're typically referring to the independent business owners we serve as our clients. We are committed to serving these clients because we recognize and appreciate how they serve us and our communities. Whether it's a craft brewery in Seattle, a chain of auto-parts retailers in Kentucky, or a bridal-store software developer based out of Georgia, independent businesses provide an essential service to our communities by creating places where people can experience the types of one-on-one, human interactions that have become all too rare in our globalized, digitized, and growth-centric economy.

Unfortunately, these businesses are typically underserved by the payments industry, which means they struggle to compete against larger and more powerful organizations with more resources at their disposal. For a multinational corporation, a 0.5 percent difference in processing fees may amount to a blip on its balance sheet; for a local boutique with one or two locations and a slim profit margin, it could mean the difference between life and death. Serving the little guy or gal business owner therefore requires us to put their needs ahead of our own, doing what is best for our clients even if it means we earn less money. It means admitting when we've made a mistake and then doing everything in our power to rectify it. It means being honest and transparent even when doing so is difficult. And it means coming up with creative solutions when the normal ways of solving a problem aren't working.

Doing these things sounds nice in theory, but they are often difficult in practice. One reason for this is because putting our clients before ourselves requires making sacrifices. Another is because there are few—if any—models for how to run a company that doesn't measure its success by profit alone.

There are two ways we keep ourselves focused on our mission, even when things get tough. First, we remember that "success" to us is not about making the most money; it's about serving the most people. By measuring our success against a different benchmark from our competitors, we force ourselves to behave in ways that reflect what we say we value.

The second way we maintain focus is by creating a culture based on a strong set of shared values. We believe that individuals rise or fall to the standard of the culture in which they operate. If your culture is built on greed and self-protection, you will become greedy and act to preserve your own self-interest; If your culture is built on trust, community, and humility, you will behave in a way that is in line with those values. By creating a strong, values-based culture, we empower our people to make decisions in line with those values—decisions that serve our clients and help the company grow without compromising our integrity.

Cultural Foundations

Our commitment to culture started in the earliest days of our company. Throughout middle and part of high school, CEO and founder Dan Price performed in a Christian punk rock band with a few of his (more talented) classmates. Because the band's members were underage and couldn't play in nightclubs and bars, they had limited choices for performance venues. Thankfully, they ended up finding a home for their band at a small coffee shop called Moxie Java in Caldwell, Idaho. The owner, Heather, not only gave them a place to perform, but also a place to build community, introduce their music to a new audience, and engage with their fans.

This experience showed Dan just how important independent businesses are to their communities. A few years later, when Dan was a senior in high school, he had a chance to return the favor to Heather and Moxie Java. In talking to Heather about her business, Dan learned that her credit card processor had recently raised her rates to the point that it was becoming a burden for her to accept credit cards. Despite knowing little about the credit card processing industry, Dan decided to help and started making phone calls to negotiate lower processing rates on Heather's behalf. He realized that people like Heather, who are focused on running their businesses on razor-thin margins and lack the resources and leverage of larger companies, get taken advantage of by processors, banks, and financial institutions all the time. He knew this was unfair and decided to do whatever he could to help level the playing field for these vital, community-supported, and independent businesses.

A couple of years later, when Dan co-founded Gravity Payments with his brother Lucas, he knew he wanted to create a credit card processing company that was different from its competitors. Having interacted with many of these processors in his role as a consultant to small businesses like Moxie Java, Dan knew that many of them cared little for the wellbeing of the businesses they served. Instead, most of them were solely focused on getting as much money as possible from small-business owners, who didn't always have the knowledge, time, or resources to know they were being taken advantage of, let alone the energy to haggle or switch to a different processor. In addition to charging high fees, some of these processors resorted to shady practices, like hiding fees from customers, raising fees without notice, or generally withholding information from clients that could affect the way they run their businesses.

As Dan built Gravity, he made serving business owners his number one priority to the point that he was willing to sacrifice money or growth in order to do so. For example, in the early days of the business, he refused to take on outside investment or venture capital that would have forced him to cede some decision-making power to investors. He knew these outsiders might not have the same goals as the business and didn't want our ability to act in the best interest of our merchants to be compromised for the sake of fast cash.

The mission statement that opened this book grew directly from Dan's early commitment to independent business owners. But since everyone has different experiences, we cannot take it for granted that every one of our team members will naturally share this philosophy. That's why we tell stories and discuss our values in order to build a shared culture in which everyone, regardless of background, can operate with clarity, intention, and purpose.

While we've practiced some of our values since the company's earliest days, others have evolved over time. For example, we've always been willing to act with integrity and transparency in an effort to serve our merchants, but it wasn't until the company started to grow that we came to understand the importance of direct feedback or giving people autonomy in order to support our clients even more.

At the same time, ==just like a high-performance sports car requires more care and maintenance than a jalopy, a high-performance, mission-driven culture requires more attention than an average one.== As we've grown, we've realized that we cannot take these values—even the ones that seem to come most naturally—for granted and assume they will always be communicated and practiced consistently throughout the company. If we want to sustain our culture over the long haul, we need tools and resources that allow us to articulate, illustrate, and enact our values so we don't lose sight of what matters most to the organization.

With this in mind, we decided to create this culture book, a document designed to codify our most important values and share stories of those values in action so we can continue to stay focused on our core mission as the company grows and evolves. Unlike an employee handbook or code of conduct, this book is not designed to dictate behavior or outline formal policies and procedures but to empower individuals with the tools they need to understand the culture to which we aspire. By outlining, explaining, and illustrating our most important values, we seek to educate and inspire those who work with our company—as employees, merchants, or partners—so we can ensure we're all working toward the same goals and adhering to the same standards.

We Are Creators, Not Consumers

While it's true that a culture will always reflect the values and actions of those in positions of power, and a strong, sustainable culture requires leadership to demonstrate and embrace it, we believe that each and every member of an organization should be able to help create the culture in which they want to work. This is a philosophy we refer to as "Creators, not Consumers."

Consumers evaluate all of the options available to them and then select the one that best suits their needs. Whether they're shopping for a new car, comparing hotels for a family vacation, or browsing online for a new pair of shoes, they'll ask certain questions before arriving at their decision: What is the price? Does it have the features I'm looking for? Does it meet more or fewer of my needs than this other option?

Most people, when looking for or working at a job, adopt this same Consumer mindset. They evaluate all of the options available to them and then pick the job or organization that meets most of their needs. "Does this job fit my skill set, interests, and career goals? Does this company value the same things I do? Does the culture align with my personality and priorities? Does it pay well? Are there opportunities for career advancement? Will I enjoy the work?" Using whatever information they have at their disposal, they'll pick the job for which they can answer "yes" to most of these questions. If, after working at a job for a certain period of time, they find it no longer meets their needs, they'll search elsewhere for a better one.

Creators, on the other hand, don't settle for the options available to them but ask how they might be able to create whatever it is they are looking for. If they are unsatisfied by the choices presented to them, Creators will make something new instead of settling for an imperfect option. This is what drives many of the entrepreneurs in our culture; they see a need that is not being filled in the market and, instead of accepting that as reality, seek to fill that need by creating something new.

When it comes to their careers, Creators will create the jobs or companies they want instead of settling for something that doesn't align with all of their needs and objectives. Instead of leaving a company because they don't like their current position, Creators will invent a role that serves the company while also satisfying their own ambitions. Instead of wishing their company was more transparent or promoted more growth and development opportunities, they take initiative in making those things happen. If they see an area where the company can improve, they speak up and take action to make a change.

Unfortunately, most companies do not value Creators because they rock the boat and cause trouble. They force people to address problems they might want to ignore and upset the order of things, which creates discomfort. Some companies may even see Creators as threats because they are unwilling to accept the status quo and therefore might challenge any authority that seeks to uphold it. Creators are, by nature, disruptive, and disruption is often viewed as an inconvenience by those who are satisfied with the way things are.

==At Gravity, we empower each and every one of our people to create the company for which they want to work.== This might sound like a recipe for chaos, but in reality we have found it creates a stronger culture by retaining talent, holding leadership accountable, and utilizing the potential of every team member.

The values presented in this book were created and articulated by our people through their actions and efforts, and we chose to present them here because our people—not just those in management, but everyone—have consistently identified them as critical toward fulfilling our core mission. That said, we recognize that different people may interpret values differently and that, over time, our culture may evolve to reflect a different set of values. The goal with this book, then, is not to dictate how one should or should not behave or present a static vision for our company going forward; it's to showcase the elements of our culture that we believe allow us to be successful while simultaneously giving each one of us the tools to create a culture of which we can be proud.

To clarify, when we say we want people to create the culture to which they aspire, we do not mean that anyone can come into our organization and dictate how it should be run. We recognize that not everyone will align with our values or support our mission, and that is fine. We understand that part of ==the benefit of having a strong culture is not simply to attract the right people, but to repel the wrong ones.== When we talk about encouraging our people to create the culture to which we aspire, we do so with the understanding that, in order for any culture to be effective, everyone must be working toward a unified purpose and goal. In our case that is to support independent business owners, and we strive to create a culture that gets better at doing that every day. Asking you to help us create this culture is our way of admitting that we are not perfect, nor do we have all the answers. It is a call to action, not a call to anarchy.

How to Use This Book

Several years ago, when discussing our most important values at a company retreat, we realized they could be summarized by three core or umbrella values: Creative Leadership, Passion for Progress, and Responsibility. While we often refer to values like "autonomy" or "transparency" or "direct feedback," we adopted the Three Core Values as a shorthand way to encompass all of the values that drive the company forward.

With this in mind, we've organized this book into four parts—one for each of the core values and a fourth that covers our unique compensation philosophy, which we consider a vital part of our culture that helps support each of our core values. Each part will define the values and elaborate on what it means to practice these values at Gravity. We will offer examples and real-life stories of these values in action so you can better understand what we mean when we discuss each of them.

We are human beings who are apt to stumble from time to time. As such the culture presented in the pages that follow is the one *to which we aspire*, not the one we claim to have today. Therefore, when we discuss the ways we put our values into practice, we are describing an *ideal*, not claiming to have perfected the standard to which we hold ourselves. So while we share many stories of our values in action, we have purposefully left out the countless examples of where we've fallen short and acted in ways counter to our values. This is not an attempt to rewrite history or obscure reality, but rather a way to visualize what's possible and provide ourselves a benchmark by which to measure our progress.

With this in mind, we hope you will use this book to hold yourselves and others accountable. In other words, this document gives you permission to speak up when you witness behavior that goes against the values described here. It also empowers you to share any ideas you may have for how we can better put our values into action.

We also hope you will use this book to reflect on how you can incorporate our values into your own life and work. At the end of each chapter, you will find questions for reflection. We urge you to think about these questions on your own time or whenever you need guidance. We also encourage you to discuss the ideas in this book with anyone else at the company and to suggest ways we can improve our culture and/or further our mission of helping the little guy and gal.

Like our culture itself, this book should be ever-evolving, changing as we change and growing as we grow. If you have questions, comments, or concerns, we encourage you to voice them to whomever is in the best position to address them. In the meantime, enjoy the book.

PART 1
CREATIVE LEADERSHIP

In early 2019, Vice President of Finance Edwin Dutton sent an email to the entire company with the subject line "*Please Read Me*: Price Increase." The body detailed a proposed $15 monthly price increase to all merchants designed to help cover increased costs and plan for the future. At many companies, an email of this nature would be purely informational—a heads up to the team that an important decision had been made and a major change was about to take place.

But Edwin's email was different. "I view this as a huge decision, and something that may appear counter to how we've operated in the past," he wrote. "I have talked through this idea with a number of people, all who had good opinions, but I realize that the majority of people haven't heard this from me. Because of that, I want to open this up as a vote in order to hear everyone's voice." He then went on to invite every team member to vote on whether they supported the increase and insisted that it would only take effect if at least 85 percent of responses were positive.

Edwin gave everyone a few days to respond and followed up with the results shortly after that. In the end, only 54 percent of respondents voted yes so the fee was not implemented and we, as a team, shifted our focus to figuring out other ways to cover our costs.

This story embodies many of our values, but it is a prime example of what we mean by Creative Leadership. ==Creative Leadership requires that we search for the best solutions to problems, no matter where those solutions come from.== It means soliciting feedback and opinions from unlikely sources, considering alternatives to the way things have been done in the past, and looking for win-win opportunities wherever they might exist. It means not letting your title or role within the company define how you contribute and behave, and it means taking ownership of problems even if you don't have a clear idea of the solution. In other organizations, a VP of finance might be empowered—even expected—to make the final decisions about a portfolio-wide price increase with little or no input from others—except, perhaps other directors or VPs—at the company. But Edwin knew that, despite his knowledge of the company and the industry, his opinion was not the only one that mattered. So he came up with a novel way to solve the problem at hand by tapping into the knowledge, experience, and creativity of the rest of the team.

Creative Leadership requires a lot of things, but it is most commonly conveyed through three qualities we aspire to at Gravity: autonomy, transparency, and a customer-centric hierarchy.

CHAPTER 1
BE YOUR OWN CEO

We believe in autonomy because we believe in trusting our employees to do the right thing. Too often, this trust is lacking within organizations, especially large ones, and results in micromanagement, siloed responsibilities, and breakdowns in communication. In a misguided effort to provide structure and order and to protect the assumed authority of those in management positions, companies that do not promote autonomy inhibit efficiency and thwart the free flow of ideas. Seeing companies limit employee autonomy makes one wonder: if you don't trust your people to do their jobs, why did you hire them in the first place?

At Gravity, autonomy is encompassed by our Be Your Own CEO philosophy. Being your own CEO means behaving as if you were the CEO or owner of the company as opposed to someone hired to a specific department or assigned a narrow job function. A CEO is responsible for making decisions that will affect all of a company's stakeholders and for sharing bold ideas to help the company and its people thrive long into the future. So even though they have immense authority, they must consider the impact of their decisions on employees, customers, and the larger community rather than acting unilaterally out of their own self-interest.

When we refer to "being your own CEO," we are referring to the fact that each team member at Gravity is empowered to solve problems and make decisions on topics for which they are accountable while simultaneously communicating those decisions and getting feedback on them from those whom will be affected. ==Being your own CEO means acting responsibly, collaboratively, and creatively. It means taking initiative and considering the big picture instead of simply focusing on the task at hand. It means being willing to take risks while simultaneously trying to mitigate those risks in the best interest of the company and our stakeholders.== As Dan Price puts it, being your own CEO means "thinking, behaving, and learning like a business owner." When Edwin solicited feedback on the proposed price increase, he was being his own CEO by exercising judgment, proposing solutions, communicating what was at stake, and asking for feedback.

At the same time, the best CEOs practice humility. They know where they excel and where they have an opportunity to make an impact, but they also know when to ask for help or to delegate a responsibility to someone else who may be better suited to the task. With this in mind, being your own CEO does not mean doing whatever you want to do or acting unilaterally. Nor does it mean ignoring the decisions of others with whom you disagree. Being a CEO is not about power or authority or being "in charge." It's about responsibility, ownership, and effective leadership.

Hayley Vogt, Digital Marketing Manager, Seattle
In early 2014, I was hired as the second member of Gravity's Marketing Team. Coming from a traditional company back in Minneapolis, I was immediately struck by the Be Your Own CEO culture. Many of my peers around me were moving fast and getting things done in a way that was efficient and hugely beneficial to the company. I wanted to be part of that.

One day I was researching business awards and stumbled upon *Entrepreneur* magazine's Entrepreneur of the Year Award. While looking through the criteria for applying, I realized each bullet point was everything Gravity and Dan Price stood for, and I knew an award like this would be a great way to get attention for the company.

I submitted an application and got an email the following week saying Dan had been selected as one of the top ten finalists. A special committee would narrow that list down to the top five based on an essay. I wrote an essay about why I thought Dan deserved the award, submitted it, and waited for a response.

Several weeks later, *Entrepreneur* emailed saying Dan had been selected as one of the top five finalists. I was thrilled, but then I read a little further and found out that, in order to continue to be considered, we had to create and submit a one-minute video about Dan and Gravity—and we had less than five business days to do it. For a two-person marketing team with limited time and resources, this was going to be a huge task. But I was determined.

I knew that Wyatt Kedinger, who was on our Deployment Team at the time, had video-editing experience. I asked him if he'd be willing to help, and he agreed. But when I discussed the opportunity with my boss, Ryan Pirkle, and Dan, they said they didn't think it was worth spending time and resources to produce the video. I pushed back. I told them that, even if we didn't win the award, we could use the video on our website. They were still resistant, but when it became clear that I was determined and had a plan in place, they relented.

Over the next few days, Wyatt, Dan, and I scrambled to finish the video. We pulled it off just in time and submitted the video. *Entrepreneur* posted it on their website next to the other finalists' videos and opened the contest up for public voting. When I saw who we were up against, I thought we had no chance of winning, but I was wrong. A few weeks later, *Entrepreneur* emailed to tell us Dan had won! A few months after that, he appeared on the cover of the magazine, and that coverage provided Gravity a level of exposure that still benefits us to this day.

About a year later, Ryan told me one of the reasons he let me make the video even though he didn't think it was a good idea is because he thought it would teach me a lesson about failure and prioritizing my time. We're both glad he was wrong, but I'm also glad to work for a place that allows me to take risks and try things I am passionate about. That's what being your own CEO is all about.

A Mindset, Not a Title

When someone proposes a new project or solution to a problem, you'll often hear people at Gravity refer to them as the "CEO" of that project. This is our way of communicating that someone has stepped up and taken charge of a particular task, but the phrase "Be Your Own CEO" describes a much broader mentality. Even if you're not currently the designated "CEO" of something, we expect you to be operating with a CEO mindset. This means you are constantly looking for things that can be improved and taking steps to improve them. It means questioning the way something is done even if it's always been done that way. It means asking questions, seeking information, and staying curious. It means building relationships with your coworkers and customers to better understand their needs and concerns. It means investing in your own growth and development so you can become a more effective and engaging leader.

Being your own CEO might involve leading a major project like developing a new product or building a new team from scratch. Or it may involve something less dramatic, like reevaluating your department's expenses to see if there's a way to save some money.

> **Mitch Esplin, Integration Specialist, Boise**
> One of the first things I noticed when joining Gravity was the Be Your Own CEO concept and the amount of autonomy it brings with it. Not only am I trusted to do my job on a daily basis, but I'm also able to go the extra mile to serve our merchants without anyone questioning the decision. For example, I love traveling to visit merchants, especially if they're having problems or could just use some extra attention. Even though I'm based in Boise, I can book a trip to Boston if a merchant there needs my help. In fact, I've flown all over the country just so I could be there on the ground to fix a problem.
>
> In recent years, I've also started visiting merchants when I'm traveling to their area for another reason—typically an industry conference. In early 2018, I even extended a trip to Denver after I learned that a merchant there was having persistent issues with their system. I knew the conference I was attending in the area would take up all the time I'd planned to stay, so I changed my flight to fly in a couple days early, and no one questioned the decision. In fact, I'm not even sure I mentioned to anyone that I was doing it; I just knew it wouldn't be a problem.

> I spent several hours with that merchant, and several months later I ran into the owner at another conference in Chicago. He told me he was super grateful that I'd flown to see them in person and that they hadn't had any problems since. It makes me feel good to be able to serve our merchants in this way and to be able to use my own judgement to make decisions that help our company and the people we work for.

Our people practice being their own CEO in ways both big and small. For instance, when a Sales Rep comes up with a creative solution for a new client, they are behaving like a CEO in that interaction. Likewise, if someone wants to spearhead a new project or initiative they feel is important, they become the CEO of that project by presenting their idea to relevant parties, getting buy-in from those who will be affected, doing the legwork to move the project forward, and holding themselves accountable for completing the project efficiently.

The best CEOs are team players who know both how to leverage their strengths to have an impact and when to step aside to let someone with a different set of skills shine. Knowing this, it's important to have a good sense of self-awareness as well as a healthy dose of confident humility, i.e. an awareness of your strengths and weaknesses and how they might affect your team.

> **Michael Margulis, Sales, San Diego**
> One of the accounts I am most proud to work with is a chain of vitamin and supplement stores based in Southern California. What makes this client so special is the fact that the owner is a former Marine and, since there are a ton of military bases in and around San Diego, the vast majority of his clients are in the military. When I first started talking to this owner about possibly switching to us as his processor, I was excited at the prospect of being able to serve someone who has dedicated his life to serving our military, both

through his own service and as an entrepreneur.

After analyzing the statements from his current processor, I could see that he was getting a bad deal on his rates, so it was pretty easy to offer him a better deal. But I wanted to do more. I noticed that a lot of the equipment he used was very old and not user-friendly. This complicated things for both his staff, who had trouble figuring out how to use the various machines, and his customers, who had to wait while the staff checked them out. This inefficiency was costing him money by making it harder for customers to shop in his stores. So, with the help of a couple of my colleagues, I put together a fully customized solution that upgraded his system and gave his shop a fresh new look. We also trained each of his staff members on the new system and helped the owner streamline his website so he could reach even more customers online. Not only did these improvements improve productivity, they also made the stores look and feel more professional, which, as a former entrepreneur myself, I know can make a huge difference to a business owner.

Not only did we end up saving this client between $12,000-$15,000 a year across all of his locations, but we also developed a close relationship with him by showing him that we genuinely cared about his business. At most credit card processors, the sales process is driven by the desire to sign as many clients for as much money as possible. But, because I was allowed to be my own CEO, I knew I was empowered to do what I thought was best, not just for my company, but for my client as well.

We encourage people to develop this self-awareness by giving them tools and resources to explore their personalities, develop their skills, and identify room for improvement. We do this through regular feedback, training and development classes, and personality assessments such as DISC. We also encourage a Be-Your-Own-CEO culture by eliminating unnecessary hurdles that can interfere with an individual's ability to work in a way that best suits them. For example, we offer flexible work schedules and open paid time off because we believe people work more effectively when they are treated like adults who can be trusted to manage their own time effectively. We also discourage micromanagement and encourage individuals to have conversations with their managers about their goals, preferences, and ideas.

We encourage you to take the time to assess your own strengths and weaknesses, as well as your goals, so you can better understand how to best contribute to our team. Are you better at strategic, big-picture thinking or executing on someone else's ideas? Do you consider yourself more creative or analytical? Do you enjoy working with people or do you prefer to handle data and facts? If you need help assessing your strengths, you can refer to the "Strengths and Weaknesses" chapter of *Equip*, Gravity's leadership book. Once you understand how your unique qualities can contribute to the team, talk to your manager about how to tailor your role so you can be most effective.

Diego Sierra, Sales, South Sound
One of the first merchants I signed was a small sandwich shop in Yelm, a town about two hours outside of Seattle. It wasn't a huge account, and the owner was happy that we would be able to save her about $60 a month in processing fees.

Unfortunately, I didn't realize at the time that the POS system we were switching her to charged a $40 monthly software fee that negated most of those savings. A couple of weeks after signing the account, I received the survey we send to all new merchants to gauge their on-boarding experience. She had basically given me the worst score possible and said she felt I had lied to her in order to get her business. I called her up, and she was furious. I told her that I didn't know about the fee when I opened her account and apologized profusely, but she was still angry. So I drove out to her business to see if having a face-to-face conversation would help. Nothing I said made much of a difference until I had an idea.

Every week, the Seattle and Boise offices get lunch catered by one of our merchants in the area. I asked the owner if she would stick with us if we agreed to place a catering order with her once every quarter. This would amount to several thousand dollars worth of food a year for an account that only makes us about $12 in revenue each month, but it helped us keep her business and allowed me to make up for my mistake. I felt empowered to make this decision because I knew the company would stand behind me taking ownership of a problem and doing right by this merchant. Now, every few months, I drive four hours out of my way to pick up sandwiches from Ronda in Yelm, and she is very happy to be a Gravity customer. Now we have an awesome relationship and she refers clients to me on a regular basis.

Alex Franklin, Sales Recruiting, Seattle
One day soon after I was hired at the company, Dan called me up and invited me to attend a sales meeting with him at a well-known multi-location coffee shop in the area. At the end of the meeting, we told the owner we would figure out a proposal and decide what would be the best option for him going forward and schedule a time to present our findings.

I went back to the office and was able to determine pretty quickly that we weren't going to be a good fit for this merchant. In fact, we would need to charge nearly double their current rates in order to break even on the deal. Rather than communicate this hard truth directly to the merchant, I waited until I could connect with Dan. Even though I knew what the right move was for the customer, I made the mistake of waiting to make sure my boss agreed with the decision. To make the situation worse, Dan was travelling and not immediately available. Still, I waited. The next time I saw Dan—now at least a week after our original meeting — he asked me where I was in our sales process with the merchant. I told him that I wanted to connect with him and put a strategy in place. Perplexed, he asked if that meant I hadn't been in contact with the owner. After I attested to this, he acknowledged my answer and left. At the end of the day though, he asked to meet me in private. Beyond voicing his disappointment and how I had effectively let both the merchant and Gravity down, he communicated an important part of our culture: I didn't need to get approval to move forward with decisions that were clearly in the best interest of the merchant.

At Gravity it doesn't matter how much experience you have or what your title is, you are still responsible for owning both action steps and outcomes, all while exhibiting a bias for action.

Being one's own CEO looks different for everyone. Some people are natural leaders who get excited by coming up with big ideas and getting people to support them. Others might take a more heads-down approach, choosing to make an impact in small but direct ways through their day-to-day decision making and actions. Ultimately, being your own CEO is less about what you do and how you do it and more about looking within yourself to develop your own leadership strengths.

Questions for Reflection

1. What is something you'd like to change at Gravity? Is there a process that could be improved? A product that could be developed? A new role or job function that needs to be filled?

   _____
   _____
   _____

2. What could you do to help make this change happen? Who would you need to talk to? What resources would you need?

   _____
   _____
   _____

3. Think about a decision you made recently that had a positive impact on the company. What inspired you to make this decision? How did you make it happen? What were the results?

   _____
   _____
   _____

CHAPTER 2
TRANSPARENCY

Effective leaders make decisions by marshalling data and facts and using them to make informed decisions. Thus, in order to maintain a Be-our-Own-CEO culture and promote Creative Leadership, we encourage people to practice transparency by seeking and sharing information. Transparency can be a tricky subject because it can mean different things to different people, especially in the context of running a business. ==To us, transparency means openly sharing facts, data, stories, emotions, motivations, and perspectives with other stakeholders in your organization in an effort to help them make better, more informed decisions, establish trust, and encourage dialogue.==

We share this information because we believe our employees are confident adults who can consume a wide variety of information and put it into the appropriate context. Many companies are paternalistic in how they disseminate data, deciding what employees can "handle" and hiding the rest because they don't think their people will respond well. By contrast, we believe that trusting our people with information allows them to feel empowered and like part of a team.

This information can come in many forms, for example, an industry update that will affect a department's workflow process or communication from one department about how a new initiative or project they're taking on will affect other people at the company.

Transparency can also take the form of sharing high-level information, for example the financial status of the company or an industry shift that will affect the way we do business. While this information may not directly impact a Client Success Engineer's ability to offer great service or Development's ability to build an amazing new product, we believe this information allows our people to feel more connected to the company's goals and objectives, to give them benchmarks for how we're doing, and to better understand how their work can have a direct impact on our bottom line. We proactively share this type of information at our all-company meetings, as well as through regular email communication such as revenue reports and product updates.

Dan Price, CEO
In 2015, right around the time when our company was getting a ton of attention for the living-wage decision, my older brother and former business partner, Lucas, sued me and the company for $26 million. There was absolutely no way we could pay this, and, even if we somehow managed to win the case, I knew the cost of fighting the lawsuit in court would be a huge burden on our bottom line and potentially threaten the very existence of the company. It was an extremely scary time. On the one hand, our business was doing great and we were growing rapidly; on the other, everything our team had worked so hard for was threatened

to be wiped out in a matter of months.

Typically, when companies face a lawsuit, they provide only the most basic details to everyone else at the company. The lawsuit itself is public record, so there's no way to pretend it isn't happening, but beyond that, executives tend to share information on a strict need-to-know basis and might choose to only share updates when the court hands down new information—again stuff that's all on the public record. But I knew the livelihood of each and every one of our team members was at stake, and as painful as the whole experience was, I owed it to them to keep them apprised of the situation.

I talked to a few people at the company about my desire to share the information with everyone. While several pointed out the risks involved—for example that the news might upset or distract people and some employees might decide to look for new jobs—we all agreed our team deserved to know what was going on. We owed it to them to share information that could have a tremendous impact on their lives.

At an all-company meeting in the summer of 2015, I announced the lawsuit, and as the court proceedings played out over the next year, I sent several emails explaining where we were in the process. If nothing changed for a few months, I sometimes sent an email to say there had been no new developments. The following summer, the judge finally handed down a decision in our favor.

There are lots of things we do at Gravity that have implications on other people, and we should do everything we can to provide information that will help them make the best decisions possible. That is what we mean by transparency.

Transparency in Action

Transparency is practiced in two ways. The first is when a department or individual proactively shares information with those they think will benefit from it—for example, when Finance discloses quarterly or annual profits and losses, Development sends an all-company email about a new product feature or update, or Team Advocates (our HR team, also known as "TA") shares the reasoning behind a new company-wide policy.

The second happens when a department or individual shares information with those who seek it directly. It is not always efficient to share updates or information with everyone; If we did, people could quickly become overwhelmed or inundated, especially if they lacked the context to understand the implications of this information. Instead, we empower individuals to seek out any information they feel is important. This applies to all levels of the company and to almost any class of information—from high-level financial information to leadership decisions to information on another department's projects. As an employee of Gravity, you should always feel empowered to ask for information, and if, for whatever reason, someone is unwilling to share it with you, you are empowered to ask why. Are you curious about why the Development Team is working on a particular software upgrade instead of another? Reach out to the person in charge of the project and ask them about it. Are you alarmed by a recent announcement about our merchant attrition rate? Reach out to the person who sent the announcement to ask for additional context.

The only type of information that our commitment to transparency does not cover is that which is protected in the interest of employee privacy. For example, we as a company are not at liberty to disclose information about an employee's health, employment status, financial situation, family situation, sexual orientation, or anything else that is protected under the law. We also do not disclose other information like performance issues or employee conflicts except with those who are directly involved in order to protect privacy and limit distractions.

Transparency also works both ways. If someone asks you for information that you are in a position to share, you should feel comfortable sharing it. If you are not comfortable sharing it—perhaps because you don't feel like the right person to do so or you're not confident the information you have is accurate or complete—then you can say so. The goal is to share information and communicate openly in an effort to create a culture of trust.

Questions for Reflection

1. Is there information you don't have that would help you do your job better? If so, how can you get this information?

   _____
   _____
   _____

2. Do people often ask you for information? Do they typically ask for the same types of information? If so, would you consider proactively sharing this information with those who need it instead of waiting for them to ask?

   _____
   _____
   _____

3. When communicating with people both inside and outside of Gravity, do you ever purposely withhold information? Why or why not? What would happen if you opted to share that information instead?

   _____
   _____
   _____

CHAPTER 3
CUSTOMER-CENTRIC HIERARCHY

We've all had this experience: you have a problem with a product or service you purchased from a particular company, so you call customer service looking for assistance. If you're lucky enough to get a live human being on the phone, you explain the problem. The solution seems simple—issue a refund, send a replacement, fix whatever is broken—but the person you're speaking to doesn't have the authority to help you. You're either transferred to another person or your problem goes unsolved.

The people who work directly with customers are often the ones that understand their needs most intimately. And yet most organizations do not trust or empower those people to make decisions to help their customers. Instead, managers and directors—those "up the chain"—decide what is best and issue orders to everyone who reports to them. You see this in non-customer-facing roles as well, anytime someone is denied an opportunity to solve a problem or make a decision simply because they lack a particular title or job description.

This is absurd. Why, for starters, would you hire someone whose judgment you didn't trust? Furthermore, why wouldn't you trust the people in charge of helping customers to actually help your customers? This not only creates inefficiency and unhappy customers, but it wastes the talents and knowledge of the people who help your company succeed. Sure, you need leaders to provide guidance, support, big-picture thinking, and long-term planning. But without the people doing the actual day-to-day work that keeps your company afloat, you'd be out of business faster than you can say, "I need to speak to a manager."

==At Gravity we understand that the people who work in a particular job are best equipped to make decisions about how they do that job. As such we strive to create a customer-centric hierarchy that empowers everyone to make decisions that help the company.== While there are, by definition, layers to this hierarchy, the main thing that distinguishes managers, directors, VPs, and executives from the people who report to them is the particular role they play as opposed to the amount of authority they have.

Communication in a Customer-Centric Hierarchy

A customer-centric hierarchy promotes autonomy, transparency, Creative Leadership, and a Be-Your-Own-CEO culture because it reduces bottlenecks and bureaucracy and promotes open communication and collaboration. In a traditional top-down leadership structure, employees who aren't in management feel they must "go up the chain of command" in order to share their ideas and opinions. Under these circumstances, even brilliant ideas risk never being heard because they require multiple people to buy into and advocate for them before they reach the person in a position to act. No one can better represent an idea than the person who had the idea, which is why we want to create an organization in which every person feels empowered to share their ideas directly with those who need to hear them.

This works both up and across the organization. If one of our Client Success Engineers has an idea for restructuring the various Support departments (Client Success Engineers, Deployment, and Tech Support) in a way that will allow for faster customer response times, they can share it directly with the managers of those departments to get their feedback and figure out a way to implement the plan in a way that will work for everyone. Similarly, if that person has a suggestion for the Development Team that they think will improve the merchant experience, they can share it directly with a member of the Development Team.

At the same time, a customer-centric structure promotes open and consistent communication among all areas of the organization because it allows information to be shared directly with those who need it the most. You cannot expect someone to make sound decisions if they don't have adequate information, so we make it easy for people across the company to communicate directly with one another whenever the need arises. What happens in one department often impacts what goes on in another department, so it is vital that these departments be able to communicate quickly with one another. If someone in Finance notices discrepancies in a merchant's account, they are empowered to reach out directly to the Sales Rep or a Sales Manager to point out the issue. If a Client Success Engineer notices that a particular merchant has called several times in the past few months, they may suggest that the Sales Rep who signed the account check in with the merchant to make sure there isn't a larger issue at work.

Tammi Kroll, COO, CTO, and CIO

When I first joined the company, I didn't have a specific job description or any direct reports. So during my first few weeks, I shadowed every department and asked people what their pain points were. It became clear through observation and conversation that we desperately needed some sort of Customer Relationship Management (CRM) system that would allow us to store information on our merchants and partners in one central database. At the time, different departments were communicating mostly via email and storing information in a bunch of different systems. That may have worked fine when the company was small, but it was making communication extremely difficult and creating all sorts of errors as we grew.

I presented my recommendation to Dan and asked him what information he'd need to approve me getting started. I'd implemented similar systems during my previous jobs at large technology companies. In each case, I'd spent months doing research and putting together a presentation to make my case to the people I reported to. Implementing a CRM costs millions of dollars, so coming from the background I did, I assumed Dan would want to vet the project carefully.

I was completely blown away when Dan told me I didn't need to convince him; if the team and I thought it was the right thing to do, we had his full support. Over the next few months, I put a small team together to help figure out which software to use and how to develop it so it would work for both Sales and Operations. We worked closely with various teams to make sure we were building a product that would actually help them, and we communicated our progress along the way. Even now, a few years after the CRM went live, we continue to make updates based on suggestions from the people who work with the software.

To me, this story exemplifies what makes Gravity different

from so many other places. Not only do we empower people to do their jobs well by trusting them to make good decisions, but we're also expected to collaborate with the people who will be directly affected instead of simply telling them what's going to happen. This not only creates a more efficient and innovative company, but it also creates a culture in which every single person feels valued and respected.

The Role of Leadership

In a traditional top-down corporate environment, the most senior leaders set direction and goals for the company and then communicate that to the rest of the company. Managers, then, are tasked with holding their teams accountable for achieving results while simultaneously serving as messengers between different layers of people.

==Thanks to our customer-centric hierarchy, Gravity managers serve a very different function. Instead of being messengers, they are representatives.== They synthesize feedback from their teams, other departments, and other managers in order to help all parties succeed. They provide support and guidance to members of their teams without micromanaging or telling them how to do their jobs. And they hold themselves and others accountable for doing what they said they were going to do.

By way of example, at an all-company meeting in the Spring of 2018, a series of large group discussions helped us identify several areas that required attention from company leadership. These included things like clarification regarding the relationship between the Boise and Seattle offices, providing additional support and resources to the Support teams, and resolving disagreements within the company. Those in the best position to address these concerns volunteered to take action while Tammi Kroll, who oversees our Operations departments, took responsibility for holding them accountable by providing weekly updates on their progress. This is a perfect example of our customer-centric hierarchy at work: a group of people from all areas of the company identified problems and then worked with one another to brainstorm solutions to those problems. Certain managers or project leads then took ownership of those solutions and figured out a plan for putting them into action. Meanwhile, the head of Operations held those people accountable and regularly communicated updates with the rest of the company.

> **Jared Spears, Inside Sales, Boise**
> In early 2017, Cody Boorman on the Finance Team contacted Merchant Relations (now known as Inside Sales) and several Outside Sales Reps saying he'd been doing research into revenue trends and had found a substantial number of "negative accounts"—merchants whose pricing was structured in a way that was actually causing us to *lose* money. Cody asked us to initiate conversations with these merchants to begin re-negotiating a win-win pricing model. Some of us on the team had never worked with Cody or even met him face-to-face since he works remotely, but he had done the initial leg-work and trusted that the team could take it from there. And the conversation didn't end there. Cody continued to check in with us over the next quarter to see how we were doing, and we developed an ongoing discussion about how we could solve this issue that was costing the company money. Thanks to Cody's initiative, we were able to rectify the problem quickly and efficiently, and, to date, the recurring annual impact of this effort has amounted to more than $1 million.
> To me, this story exemplifies our open-office culture in which any individual can use whatever resources are at their disposal—including their colleagues—to help drive the company forward. I think many companies have a closed-door attitude. "You're not in my department. You're not my manager. That's not my job. I don't know you. Why are you asking me to do something?" But that is not something we see here at Gravity. When people can collaborate with

> anyone else on a project and don't feel they have to confine themselves to their job descriptions or their departments, ego is removed from our interactions, and that brings a lot of rewards. Our customer-centric hierarchy and spirit of teamwork make people more efficient and productive and allow us to generate new ideas and solve problems quickly and creatively.

How We Promote a Customer-Centric Hierarchy

If you're used to working in a top-down environment, it might take some time for you to get used to our customer-centric hierarchy, especially when you have to make a decision quickly. Knowing this, there are a few things we do to promote collaboration and communication.

The first is through the open floor plans in our Boise and Seattle offices. We specifically designed each space so that everyone would be able to sit near one another and no individual or team would be separated from the group. In a traditional office, a person's authority is directly proportional to the size of their office. By providing everyone a similar workspace, we're signaling that, regardless of our titles or roles, we are all equal.

While we hope the open office promotes organic interactions with coworkers you might not otherwise talk to regularly, we also encourage you to reach out to anyone at the company if you have a question or want to share an idea or if you're just interested in learning more about what they do. For example, if a Deployment Rep wants to better understand our products, they could invite someone on the Development Team out for coffee to pick their brain. Likewise, someone on the Marketing Team might reach out to a Sales Rep to find out how to better support partnership and sales opportunities. If someone is not sure to whom they should reach out, they are encouraged to ask. We make this easy by making the contact information of every employee available in Namely, our HR portal.

In addition, Dan Price offers weekly office hours from 11 am-12 pm Pacific Time on Mondays and Wednesdays. During these hours anyone at the company can schedule one-on-one time with him to discuss whatever is on their mind that week. These calls are an opportunity to get feedback, discuss projects, present concerns, or share ideas. Outside of these office hours, Dan encourages team members to reach out to him directly via email or phone.

In short, a customer-centric hierarchy is about empowering people and promoting communication. As the company continues to grow, we need to stay vigilant about keeping this a priority because, while larger companies necessitate more structure, they also benefit the most from a culture in which ideas can be shared at all levels.

Questions for Reflection

1. When was the last time you spoke to someone in management who wasn't your direct supervisor? What was the conversation about and what were the results?

   _____
   _____
   _____

2. Is there information you'd like to share with or a question you'd like to ask to another department? If so, what would be the best way to convey this information?

   _____
   _____
   _____

3. Think of a time you made a decision that had a direct positive impact on a merchant, your team, or the company. What empowered you to make that decision? What was the process like?

   _____
   _____
   _____

PART II
PASSION FOR PROGRESS

In 2018, we held an all-company meeting at the Seattle office. This was the first time since we'd acquired our Boise office that everyone was together in one place, and over the course of the three-day event, employees were asked to share personal stories about their lives with their coworkers—some of whom they had never interacted with before. These exercises were specifically designed to foster a sense of vulnerability and encourage understanding among team members, so it was vital that the organizers create a safe space in which people would feel comfortable sharing intimate details from their lives with one another.

Unfortunately, an administrative error compromised this sense of safety before the meeting even officially began. Since this was the first time everyone at the company had been together, TA provided name tags so people could readily identify one another. But the name tags provided featured employees' legal names instead of the ones they actually went by. While for some people, their name is largely a matter of preference, for others, like Billing Specialist Nelson Pfab, it is in an integral part of their identity. When Nelson noticed the error, they were justifiably upset. "I immediately felt let down and betrayed by the company," Nelson said when discussing the incident later. "For me, my name is not just a preference; it's something I worked hard to secure and be recognized with at work. Here I was, already apprehensive about making myself vulnerable, and now I was being presented to strangers as someone I am not."

Nelson knew from experience that TA would understand their concerns. When they had chosen to introduce their gender-neutral pronouns to the office, they had worked with TA to come up with a way to communicate the change to the rest of the company and had found them receptive and helpful. Knowing this, Nelson felt comfortable expressing their feelings about the name-tag issue and asking that it be resolved. Nelson spoke to a few other people who had been impacted by the incorrect name tags and drafted an email to Jena Miller in TA asking that the name tags be reprinted immediately.

Jena apologized on behalf of TA, acknowledged the mistake and the harm it caused, and promised to address the situation immediately. The next day TA provided everyone with new name tags, and Dan issued a formal apology at the company meeting.

"Even innocent mistakes have the potential to hurt people, and it's important to be able to point them out," Nelson says. "Having given feedback in the past, I knew I could have an open, honest conversation with those involved with no negative repercussions."

What is a Passion for Progress?

Our Passion for Progress helps drive our company forward because we are constantly striving to improve. ==Passion for Progress demands we act quickly, take risks, and accept failure as a natural component of success.== If we are to be truly passionate about progress, we need to be willing to act boldly, even in the face of criticism. We must constantly ask ourselves, "Is there a better way?" even if things are seemingly fine and changing something may rock the boat. We must not be afraid to make mistakes, but we must also accept responsibility and learn from those mistakes in order to do better next time.

As the above story about Nelson and the name tags shows, our Passion for Progress requires that we are open to both giving and receiving feedback and consistently seek opportunities to grow, learn, and improve. Our Passion for Progress also necessities a commitment to diversity and inclusion because a company in which people from all backgrounds feel comfortable sharing ideas, opinions, and perspectives is one that can assess risks and opportunities and identify challenges and solutions that those with more narrow points of view might miss.

CHAPTER 4
A CULTURE OF CANDOR

As individuals and as a company, we cannot improve if we don't know how we're doing and where we can improve. That's why giving and receiving feedback is critical to our Passion for Progress.

What Is Feedback?
Feedback is a critical response to an idea, action, or behavior designed to encourage improvement. It can be positive, constructive, or suggestive, and we encourage all types.

Positive feedback is the easiest to both give and receive, but it is important not to take it for granted, especially when it comes to managers giving feedback to their direct reports. According to responses from employee feedback surveys, many of our team members say they enjoy receiving positive, informal feedback from a manager or a colleague and that, even something as simple as an email thanking them for a job well done or a cheers in TINYpulse is enough to make them feel appreciated and respected.

Another type of feedback can come in the form of advice or a suggestion. This type of feedback can be either solicited or unsolicited. For example, if a Sales Manager proposes a new workflow for reps to use when setting up new merchant accounts, a Sales Rep might suggest adding or removing a step based on what they feel is most efficient. This type of feedback is relatively easy to give and to receive as long as there is a culture in place that supports this type of communication. At Gravity, we frequently solicit such feedback directly from team members, but we also make it clear that everyone should feel free to weigh in, even if not directly asked to do so, if they have feedback to give.

Negative or constructive feedback is the most difficult to give and receive. Even though 82 percent of employees worldwide say they appreciate receiving feedback—even negative feedback—it's rarely pleasant to be on the receiving end of criticism.[1] In a workplace setting, this type of feedback is often presented in the context of critiquing someone's performance. For example, if a manager notices that one of their reports is not performing at a high-enough level, they will need to provide critical feedback directly to that person in order to address the situation. Similarly, an employee may witness one of their coworkers behaving in a way they find objectionable or offensive and want to make their feelings known directly to that person. In both situations, the need for direct feedback is clear, but that doesn't make the act of communicating this feedback any easier.

==When considering how to communicate direct feedback—especially critical feedback—keep in mind that, by doing so, you are doing yourself, your team, and the company==

---

[1] "Employee Feedback: The Complete Guide," Officevibe,

==a tremendous service by providing an opportunity for improvement and growth.== Without receiving feedback on where we can improve, we'll never know how to improve, and that is a disservice to everyone. "Even though feedback can be difficult to hear and I may not agree with all of it," Bobby Powers, Head of Learning and Development, says, "I've found that there's always a nugget of truth in any feedback I receive. When others share feedback with me, I get a view into how my actions are being perceived by others, which is a view that is impossible for me to otherwise see."

How We Create a Culture of Feedback

In corporate America, leaders often pay lip service to feedback. They say they value it, but when they receive it, they either ignore it or punish the person giving it. Knowing this, we—as individuals and as a company—strive to encourage feedback not just through our words, but through our actions. We do this in three primary ways:

1. Soliciting Feedback: Whenever possible, we solicit direct feedback from team members. We can do this before we take a specific action, after taking the action, or both. For example, when planning an all-company meeting in 2018, the organizers asked all team members to provide feedback on structure, goals, and activities, both before and after the meeting took place. The early feedback allowed for better execution and also more confidence among all team members in the purpose and structure of the meeting itself. The post-meeting feedback showed us where we fell short and gave us insights that will allow us to improve any future events of this nature.

While it is not always possible or appropriate to solicit direct feedback, you should consider doing so if your action or idea will affect other team members or if the success of the action or idea requires other team members to support it. For example, a

---

https://www.officevibe.com/employee-engagement-solution/employee-feedback.

manager could institute a new workflow they think will improve efficiency on their team, but by soliciting feedback in advance, rather than simply announcing the new process, they will have a better chance of creating a system that works for everyone.

In addition to soliciting feedback on a case-by-case basis, we have instituted several processes and procedures that encourage people to provide feedback. For example, we send out anonymous TINYpulse surveys each week that ask for feedback on a specific facet of the company. In addition, we conduct employee feedback interviews with every employee at least once a year. These interviews are designed to get feedback from each person on how they think the company and their department is faring, where they see room for improvement, and what opportunities they see for themselves, their teams, and the company for the future. We also conduct Manager 360 surveys, in which those who work directly with a specific manager can provide feedback on that manager's performance, as well as an annual all-company survey in which every team member has the chance to share their feedback about company goals, priorities, performance, and objectives.

2. Acting on Feedback: The most straightforward way to indicate that you take feedback seriously is to acknowledge and implement it. For example, in late 2018 TA sent out a TINYpulse question that asked "What drives you crazy here and decreases your productivity?" After several people responded that noise in the Seattle office causes distraction and interrupts their work, Bobby Powers and Lauren West in TA and Yuri Prater in IT set up some designated quiet desks on the third floor where people can go if they need to work without interruption.

Before you act on feedback, it might be necessary to get more information. Engaging the person giving feedback in a conversation will not only give you clarity on what they are suggesting, but will also communicate to the giver that their feedback is being taken seriously. For example, if someone gives you critical feedback on a presentation you gave in a team meeting, you might ask for suggestions on what you could have done better. Or if someone presents an idea for a new process that could improve interdepartmental communication, call them up to discuss how they see that process working and who else might need to be involved in the conversation. You can also share the feedback with others to see what they think and let the person giving the feedback know that you are taking their suggestions seriously.

It is, of course, impossible to implement every single piece of feedback you receive, no matter how well-intentioned it is or how much you might want to. For example, you might receive conflicting feedback from two different parties or someone might suggest a course of action that is simply not feasible due to lack of resources. At the same time, you might have information or insight into a situation that leads you to decide that someone else's suggestion is not appropriate in a given situation.

Regardless, it is important to act on all feedback you receive, even if you are not in a position to implement it. The simplest way to do this is to acknowledge the feedback and communicate with the person who gave it regarding why you're not implementing it. Even better, open up the conversation to see if there's an alternative that could work for everyone. Remember, the goal is to show that you take feedback seriously.

And if you give someone feedback that is not acted on, don't hesitate to ask for an explanation.

3. Rewarding Feedback: By rewarding those who give feedback, you communicate to those around you that feedback is welcome and that they should not be afraid of giving it, even if it is uncomfortable. Too often, employees fear they will be reprimanded or punished for offering their opinions, especially if that opinion differs from that of the majority. By thanking people openly for providing feedback or otherwise acknowledging their contributions in a public way, you remove this fear from the culture. For example, at an all-company meeting, Dan led several large group discussions in which individuals were encouraged to share their feedback on things like company values, the effectiveness of leadership, and where we could improve. Knowing that many people might find the prospect of speaking their minds in front of dozens of their coworkers—not to mention company leadership—daunting, Dan created a safe space by openly thanking individuals who shared their insights—even if those insights were in direct contrast to others' opinions or were openly critical of other people in the room. In addition, Dan encouraged people to reach out to him directly at any point to offer feedback or discuss ideas.

While we strive to create a culture in which everyone feels comfortable sharing feedback openly, we understand that, sometimes, the best way to make people feel comfortable going on record is by giving them the option to go off record. For this reason, we provide opportunities to give anonymous or off-the-record feedback when possible. One vehicle is through TINYpulse, though employees can also communicate their confidential feedback to TA, who are in a position to help them figure out the best way to make sure their feedback is considered.

Bobby Powers, Head of Learning and Development, Seattle
I started at the company in November 2017 as a Business Analyst on the Finance Team. I had heard about our company's focus on direct communication and feedback many times, but I really got to see those values in action shortly after I started.

At that time, we had a company call every Friday morning. Every team lead would give a quick update on their team's priorities and what the team had recently accomplished. The updates were intended to be quick recaps to keep everyone at the company in the loop.

On one particular call, a couple things happened that I thought could have been handled better, so I decided to give feedback to the relevant individuals. I talked to the person who shared the Marketing update and told her I didn't find the update very effective because she read the notes directly off the slides and didn't provide context on why the projects were important. To my disbelief, she thanked me profusely for that feedback. She was relatively new at the company, too, and told me she loved getting feedback because it made her better and she was always looking for ways to improve.

Similarly, I talked to the head of our Deployment Team after the call. I told him that some of the language he used in his section could have been interpreted as devaluing team members' contributions. Rather than responding in frustration, he nodded his head and said I was right. He said he hadn't considered that people could interpret his message that way and thanked me for letting him know.

In most companies, no one would listen to feedback from a Business Analyst who had just joined the company. I had no positional clout in our organization whatsoever. Yet these team members/leaders not only listened to me, but they also thanked me for talking to them. That's pretty incredible.

Feedback is a Two-Way Street

In order for a culture of feedback to work, each and every team member must be prepared to both give and receive feedback. An entry-level employee should feel just as empowered to give feedback to their coworkers, managers, and company leadership as the CEO feels giving feedback to direct reports. On the other hand, the CEO has a responsibility to receive feedback from anyone willing to give it, just as new hires expect to receive performance feedback from their managers. In fact, those in leadership stand to gain the most from direct feedback because they are in the greatest position to act on it and effect change.

How to Handle Critical Feedback

One of the biggest threats to feedback is poor communication, especially when it comes to negative or critical feedback. People avoid giving critical feedback because they aren't confident they can do so effectively. They worry their emotions will get in the way or that they will hurt someone else's feelings. On the receiving end, people might not respond well to feedback because they perceive it as a personal attack on their character as opposed to a suggestion to improve a particular behavior.

Fortunately, there are a few things you can do to improve your ability to both give and receive feedback.

1. Assume Positive Intent: Assuming positive intent requires you to consider that, even if you think someone is acting ineffectively or problematically, they have good intentions or even reasons for doing so. Assuming positive intent is the difference between assuming that guy cut you off in traffic because he's an inconsiderate jerk and assuming he did so because he's late for an important appointment or rushing to the hospital to visit a sick friend.

One should assume positive intent when both giving and receiving feedback. For example, if you are a manager who notices one of your reports is not meeting their deadlines or goals, you can assume they are lazy, or you can give them the benefit of the doubt. Perhaps there is something going on in their personal life that might be distracting them from work. Or perhaps they need clarity on something but don't know how to ask for help. The outcome in these scenarios is the same (declining productivity), but the intention is very different. Even if neither scenario is true, entering into a conversation with a more generous perspective will allow for a less tense, more productive conversation about how to improve productivity. On the other hand, if you receive critical feedback from your manager, you'll be much more likely to take the feedback constructively if you assume your manager is giving you feedback because they want you to succeed, not because they want to make you feel bad or lack confidence in you.

2. Stick to the Facts: When you approach someone with facts instead of opinions or assumptions, you set the tone for a productive conversation. If a coworker makes a remark you find offensive and you want to point it out to them, they will be much less likely to get defensive if you say, "I don't know if you're aware, but that term is a racial epithet and might offend some people," than they would be if you called them a racist in front of their peers. Similarly, when providing feedback on performance, it's much more constructive to say, "I've noticed your numbers are down from last quarter, and I'd like to find out why" rather than, "Why have you been slacking off recently?"

3. Define Mutual Purpose: Remember, the goal of feedback is to help another person or the organization improve. When we remember that we are all working toward the same goal, it becomes easier to both give and receive feedback. If you are giving critical feedback, take the time to define your mutual purpose with the person receiving the feedback as it applies to the specific situation. For example, if you are providing feedback to one of your direct reports about their performance, you might start the conversation by saying something like, "I see a lot of potential in you, and I want to do what I can to help you reach that potential," or "I've noticed your performance has not been as strong in the past couple of months as it was previously, and I'd like to see how we can work together to address any challenges you might be facing." If you're communicating with the head of another department, you might say, "Several members of my team have told me they do not feel they are getting what they need from your team in order to do their jobs effectively. I'd like to have a conversation about where the breakdown might be and what my team might be able to do to help improve communication going forward." Acknowledging mutual purpose immediately turns the other person into an ally instead of an adversary and allows you to keep an open mind and cooperate instead of becoming defensive.

While learning how to give and receive direct feedback effectively can be difficult—especially if you're not used to doing so and/or come from a company culture in which feedback was discouraged—over time, these conversations lead to a stronger, more transparent, more trusting, and more collaborative work environment. It also creates stronger, more creative, and more resilient individuals. For more information on giving and receiving feedback, check out the resources listed in Appendix A of this book.

Questions for Reflection

1. Think about a time in the past week where you had an opportunity to provide feedback. Did you? Why or why not?

   _____
   _____
   _____

2. When was the last time you provided direct feedback to someone? How successful do you feel the interaction was? Are there things you could have done differently to improve the way the feedback was communicated?

   _____
   _____
   _____

3. What are the biggest barriers to you providing feedback? How would you behave differently if those barriers didn't exist? What could you do to remove those barriers?

   _____
   _____
   _____

4. How did you respond the last time someone gave you feedback? Did you accept the feedback at face value or get defensive? If the latter, what might you have done differently to be more open and neutral to receiving the feedback? What will you do differently next time?

   _____
   _____
   _____

CHAPTER 5
WE HIRE PEOPLE, NOT RESUMES

Before Kaitlynn Vincent started working as a Sales and Operations Assistant in our Boise office, she worked in a leasing office at a local apartment complex. Referred by a former staff member, she didn't even know what the company did when she interviewed for the position. Instead, she exhibited tenacity and a passion for fighting for the little guy or gal, which indicated she'd be a great addition to the team.

Kaitlynn quickly mastered her role and impressed anyone who worked with her. So when our Boise Tech Support team was looking for a new supervisor in the summer of 2018, several people encouraged Kaitlynn to apply. She had only been with the company for three years, had never managed anyone, and lacked technical experience, but that didn't matter. She had proven her ability to learn quickly, adapt to change, work with people, and solve problems, which were the most important qualities needed for a job as fast-paced and challenging as Tech Support. She took over as Tech Support Supervisor in June 2018 and immediately stepped up to the role, helping to improve processes and communication to make the team more effective. "One of the reasons I love working here is because, if you're willing to work for them, opportunities will be given to you," Kaitlynn says. "You have to be ready to work your butt off for sure. It's not an easy ride. It's not a cake walk, and if you have that mentality, it's not going to be fun for you. But if you work hard and help people, this company is full of opportunity. Every day is an opportunity."

Hiring the Right People

Many Gravity employees started at the company without any formal experience in the payments industry or even the roles for which they were hired. We've also seen many people switch career tracks within the company during their tenures. That's why we pride ourselves in hiring people, not resumes.

A resume is a static list of skills and experiences that illustrates whether a person is appropriate for a specific job. It does not, however, represent everything that person has to offer, nor does it convey that person's full potential. It is a document that shows what is or what was, not what could be.

When we hire people, we take their specific skills and experiences into account, but mostly we consider the individuals themselves. Will they be a good fit for the company? Do they seem to want to grow and work hard? Are they eager to learn? Do we think they can provide value to the company beyond what is listed in their formal job description?

This is not only a more empathetic, humane way of hiring—one that considers applicants to be people as opposed to resources—it also makes good business sense. When you hire the right people and allow them to grow and develop, you not only increase their potential but also the potential of the company. In the book *Good to Great,* author Jim Collins writes that one of the biggest differences between good companies and great companies is that great companies ask "First who, then what."[2] In other words, good companies figure out where they want to go and what they want to do and then find people to fill the necessary roles. But great companies find the right people first and then use those people to help determine direction. Finding the right people and then giving them the tools to develop will allow the company to grow in ways you might not even be able to anticipate.

You can always teach the right people what they need to know to do a specific job or task, which is why we focus on hiring the right people first and then providing them with the tools and resources they need to thrive in the role. When we interview job candidates, there are several questions we try to answer:

- Is this person a Creator or a Consumer?
- Does this person demonstrate an ability to solve problems creatively and effectively?
- Is this person curious? Do they seek to understand the "why" behind what we do as opposed to just the "what" or "how?"
- Does this person hold themselves accountable for their own actions and learn from their mistakes?
- Does this person practice confident humility? In other words, do they know where they do and do not excel? Can they be their own CEO?
- Has this person demonstrated an ability to take risks and initiative as opposed to waiting to be told what to do?
- Is this person comfortable giving direct, honest feedback?
- Is this person passionate about serving others?

---

[2] Jim Collins, "First Who...Then What," in *Good to Great: Why Some Companies Make the Leap...and Others Don't* (New York, HarperCollins, 2001), 41-64.

If we can answer "yes" to the above, we can be confident the candidate will be an asset to our team because they will be willing to learn, adapt, and take initiative in ways that will push our company forward. Upon hiring such people, we promote their growth and development by giving them the tools they need to learn the job.

A Culture of Learning

In her book *Mindset,* psychologist Carol Dweck introduced the concept of fixed mindsets and growth mindsets.[3] People who have a fixed mindset believe people are born with a certain natural aptitude for various things and that these qualities remain pretty much fixed throughout their lives. People are either intelligent or they're not. They're disciplined or they're not. They're athletic or they're not. They're creative or they're not.

On the other hand, people with a growth mindset believe that while you may be born with certain natural abilities, these abilities can be improved with practice. In other words, you can learn to be more intelligent or a better runner or a more talented violinist, even if you're not inherently gifted in those areas.

Because they believe talent is inherent, people with fixed mindsets tend to lose confidence or interest in a task when it becomes challenging. If they perform poorly on a project, they'll think "I'm stupid," or "I'm just not cut out for this!" People with a growth mindset, however, will tell themselves, "I need to do better next time," or "I made some mistakes, but I learned from them so the experience was still valuable." Over time, people with growth mindsets tend to outperform those with fixed mindsets because they don't give up as easily and enjoy the process of learning, growth, and development.

---

[3] Carol Dweck, *Mindset: The New Psychology of Success* (New York: Ballantine Books, 2008).

At Gravity, we have a growth mindset and we try to instill one in each of our team members as well. We believe that as long as people have the right resources and a willingness to learn, they can master any task, no matter how daunting or complicated. We promote this thinking by giving people opportunities to stretch themselves through things like cross-training and internal job opportunities as well as by promoting a culture of learning through things like onboarding and skills training; leadership development training; and individualized career plans.

Craig Cooley, Technical Support Analyst, Boise
Before I came to Gravity, I'd spent most of my career in retail but realized that my favorite part of my job was fixing my computer whenever it broke. I thought I might want to work in technology, but I didn't know where to start. I didn't have an engineering degree, and I'd never worked in technology before. When a friend told me about an open position on the Tech Support Team, I decided to apply in the hope that it could be a way for me to gain some experience in the field.

After I started, I mentioned to one of our Developers, Tyler Samples, that I was interested in learning how to code. I asked for his advice on how to get the skills I needed to eventually become a developer, and he suggested starting with a small project. I'm not the best at school, so I wanted to teach myself, and this seemed like a good way to learn. I decided to build a log parser—a relatively simple technology that would allow our team to better sort and analyze data on our transaction logs. I started developing the parser on my own but soon recruited Gil Perez and James Kemp from our Tech Support Team to help out after I learned they were both interested and had some experience in coding as well.

The process allowed me to learn a lot about coding while also giving me the chance to make something that would help my team. I'm really grateful to work for a place that gives people the resources and encouragement to pursue their passions and develop their skills. In addition to working on the log parser project, I also spoke to our Director of Engineering about what I would need to do if I wanted to become a developer at Gravity. She suggested getting certified in a few particular skills by taking online courses, so I'm currently working on that in my own time.

It's amazing to me that our head of engineering would take the time to mentor a new person on a different team and in a completely different office in this way. It's also amazing that I can be so open about my interests and goals and the people around me are willing to help me achieve them. At Gravity it doesn't matter if you lack formal education or training. If you're willing to learn and put in the work, the opportunities here are endless.

Onboarding and Skills Training

All new hires undergo a formal onboarding and training process, which includes one-on-one training, job shadowing, and group training conducted in a "cohort" of other new hires. This training starts with an overview of our company values and culture, followed by a multi-day cohort training in our Seattle office wherein new hires learn about how all of the departments of the company work together to provide world-class service to merchants and partners. During cohort training, new employees also learn the basics of the credit card processing industry and how our Be-Your-Own-CEO environment encourages each person to think like a business owner. Many new hires also have the opportunity to visit our Boise office to learn about the integrated processing side of our business and meet the teams who handle integrations.

Beyond the formal training process, new hires are equipped with resources, such as Litmos (our e-learning platform) and Salesforce, in which they can find information, videos, and knowledge articles on specific aspects of the industry or company departments.

We also encourage people to cross-train in other departments if they are interested in learning more about the company. You may decide to cross-train because you want to explore specific career opportunities in another department or simply because you want to gain a better understanding of that department's role within the company. For example, Client Success Engineers and Deployment Reps often opt to cross-train with the other department since they work so closely together.

Short of formal cross-training, you are also invited to shadow someone in another department in an effort to gain insight into their work. For example, employees can elect to shadow someone in Sales or any of the operational teams to gain a better understanding of how our business operates and the challenges we face on a day-to-day basis.

Jose Garcia, Lead Culture Consultant, Boise
Before coming to Gravity, I spent several years working in the foreclosure and underwriting departments of a large national bank where most of my clients were Hispanic. When I finally quit that job and started looking for a new career, I thought my only marketable skill was my ability to speak Spanish, which, thankfully turned out to be pretty useful. I got a job on the Gravity Support Team (as it was known at the time), and the first few months were extremely intense as I learned the ins and outs of credit card processing. I'd say it took me a solid six months to learn how to do my job, but I also learned a lot about myself along the way and realized I had a lot more to offer than I'd thought. For one, I realized I had the ability to use my own judgment to make good decisions and, for the first time ever, I felt confident doing so.

As my confidence grew, I began to look for other

opportunities at the company, and my manager and I figured out a plan under which I started working in Deployment a few days a week. Several months later, when a supervisor position opened up in the department, my co-workers encouraged me to apply for it even though I was one of the least experienced people vying for the job. I somehow ended up getting the position, and even though it took me a while to adjust to being a manager, I eventually learned through trial, error, and sheer necessity how to handle the role.

The experience was extremely challenging, but it also prepared me for my next role at the company, one I was extremely passionate about. When Gravity acquired our Boise office in 2017, I knew there was going to be a lot of work involved in bringing the companies together and making sure that everyone felt like part of the same organization. I talked to Tammi about how I might be able to help, and she offered to send me to Boise where I would be in charge of integrating the two company cultures. It was a huge responsibility, but thanks to everything I'd learned at Gravity, I felt up to the challenge.

Learning and Development Training

In keeping with our Be-Your-Own-CEO philosophy, we strive to develop leaders, not just competent workers. Beyond basic skills or industry training, we also offer all employees the chance to develop broader career and leadership skills that will help them be effective in whatever jobs they have or want to pursue. These include trainings about delegation, communication, giving and receiving feedback, time management, identifying opportunities, improving productivity, and a variety of other things.

The main way in which we help employees develop these skills is through our Learning and Development University (LDU) program. We typically offer two LDU courses per month for employees, and each training is run by someone who is an expert in the specific topic (typically another team member). These training sessions are offered during the work day, and anyone is invited to participate. All classes are recorded and posted on Litmos for those who cannot attend the day-of session.

In addition to LDU, we also host lunch and learns and guest speakers who speak on a wide variety of topics. For example, in 2018, behavioral scientist and author Daniel Pink visited our Seattle office to talk about the "science of timing" and activist and author DeRay McKesson spoke to the team about what it takes to effect change at a societal level. We also encourage continuous individual learning through a company book club, a lending library at the Seattle and Boise offices, a recommended reading list (see Appendix A), and the #learning Slack channel.

Individualized Career Paths

In keeping with our philosophy of hiring people for the company, not just for a specific job, we encourage people to create their own career trajectories within the company, regardless of what department or position they were originally hired for.

At most companies, a career path is laid out for you depending on where you start. You might get hired as a Marketing assistant and then, assuming you perform well in that role, you'll receive regular promotions until you become a manager, department head, or vice president. While opportunities for advancement within a department exist at Gravity, we don't want any employee to feel limited by the job they have today. If you currently work in one department but want to explore opportunities in another, we encourage you to reach out to your manager and the head of the other department. Similarly, if you think the company would benefit from a role or department that doesn't yet exist, you can discuss these opportunities with your manager and company leadership. This sort of initiative on the part of individual employees is what led to the creation of several departments, including the Client Success Team and Demand Generation Team.

We believe in creating opportunities for our people because we know that, when people have opportunities to grow and develop in their careers, they are more engaged in their jobs, and when employees are more engaged, the entire organization benefits.

Rosita Barlow, Sales Training Development, Seattle and Boise
After I graduated college, I turned down a pretty well-paying job as a marketing coordinator because I knew it wasn't the right job for me. I wanted to pursue opportunities that would allow me to use my degree, which was in finance, so I started searching for jobs in that field. Unfortunately, this was 2006, when the market was saturated with people looking to get into finance, so I had a hard time finding a good gig.

I eventually found a job posting on Craigslist for a data-entry position at Gravity and decided to apply. I got the job but quickly found that I didn't have enough to do, so I started looking for ways to make myself useful. In my first year at the company, I learned how to install credit card terminals, assess risk for new merchant accounts, field support calls, and do payroll. Eventually, I became an Operations Manager, overseeing Underwriting, Accounting, Risk, Deployment, and what was then Support (now Client Success Engineers). I also started doing a little finance work on the side.

Eight years later, Dan suggested I move into sales management even though I had absolutely no experience in sales and wasn't confident I could grow and inspire the team. Clearly, Dan saw something in me that I didn't because I took on the role and have been in Sales ever since.

The Power of Deep Work

When you work in a fast-paced environment, your days can easily be consumed by a seemingly endless stream of tasks that may or may not be important. Yes, if a merchant is experiencing an outage and can't process, you'll need to drop everything to help them as quickly as possible. But there are plenty of other things that come up that capture your attention even if they don't deserve it. How many times, for example, have you immediately responded to a Slack message or email from a coworker even though the message wasn't that urgent? How often do you look at your to-do list at the end of the day only to discover you accomplished none of the important work you had set out to do? How often do you feel like you're not making progress even though you're working hard all day?

Our commitment to our merchants and partners is our first priority, and it's important for us to respond quickly to their needs. This customer urgency sometimes bleeds into other non-urgent work, making it feel as if we need to respond to every email and Slack message within minutes. Unfortunately, when everything seems urgent, it's easy to lose sight of other important work. It's imperative for us to prioritize things that are important but not as urgent, like cleaning up information in Salesforce, conducting an audit of negative accounts, or improving the training process for new hires on our team. These projects may never scream loudly for our attention, but they can help us make big, long-term improvements to our business.

Deep work is defined as work that is both challenging and important. Deep work generally requires a significant amount of mental energy, so it cannot be completed amidst distractions. It's the type of work that can't be completed in the fifteen minutes between meetings or while you're trying to answer emails. While it's ultimately up to each team member to set aside deep-work time in their schedule, we as a company offer several incentives and perks to encourage them to do so. For example, we allow all of our employees the opportunity to work from home our outside the office in consultation with their manager. We also offer quiet space in our Seattle and Boise offices where you can work without interruption from coworkers. We've also conducted several LDU sessions on topics like time management, flow, and prioritization to give you the tools you need to be more productive and accomplish your goals in a way that best suits your needs.

Questions for Reflection

1. What are your career goals? What can you do in your role at Gravity to help you reach those goals?

   _____
   _____
   _____

2. Think of a skill you would like to develop in your career. What resources do you need to develop those skills? Are any of them available at Gravity? Have you discussed developing these skills with your manager?

   _____
   _____
   _____

3. What parts of your job excite you the most? How can you integrate more of those things into your workday?

   _____
   _____
   _____

4. What are some long-term projects you'd like to complete? How can you incorporate deep work into your schedule to get them done?

   _____
   _____
   _____

CHAPTER 6
DIVERSITY AND INCLUSION

At Gravity, diversity and inclusion are not buzzwords but an integral part of our culture that directly supports our three core values, especially our Passion for Progress. A commitment to diversity and inclusion promotes a Passion for Progress by acknowledging that the world is changing and that, if we don't evolve to keep up with this change, we will be left behind. Research has shown that diverse companies are more innovative and productive than those that don't value diversity and inclusion.[4] The more diverse perspectives and opinions that are shared, the less likely an organization will succumb to groupthink or homogenous thinking and the more likely it will be to come up with creative solutions and ideas.

More importantly, we promote diversity and inclusion because we want to be part of the solution in helping to right some

---

[4] David Rock and Heidi Grant, "Why Diverse Teams are Smarter," *Harvard Business Review*, November 4, 2016, https://hbr.org/2016/11/why-diverse-teams-are-smarter.

of the wrongs done against certain groups in our society. For much of Western history, certain individuals have faced discrimination as a result of their identity. Historically, women, people of color, members of the LGBTQ communities, followers of certain religions, those with disabilities or mental health issues, and other minority groups have fewer opportunities and experience more prejudice than those in the majority. This is especially evident in the workplace where minorities typically earn lower salaries, have a harder time getting hired and promoted, and generally experience biases and circumstances that make it more difficult for them to succeed at work.

As an employer, we want to create a space where anyone, regardless of background, can thrive. Our living wage policy has helped correct some historical inequalities, but there's a lot more we can do. We hope our example will not only benefit the lives of those who work for us, but also set an example to other companies about what's possible when they make diversity and inclusion a priority.

James Pratt, Vice President of People Development, Seattle
In 2014, I was diagnosed with bipolar II disorder. Bipolar disorder is characterized by periods of mania and depression, and although I have held many jobs throughout my career, including a few in management, the depression part of my disorder can sometimes make it difficult for me to function, especially in a work environment. At the same time—despite the fact that most people will experience some sort of mental health problem in their life—there is still a lot of stigma and misunderstanding around mental health issues in our culture.

At previous jobs, I had often kept my bipolar disorder a secret from managers and colleagues because I worried they would treat me differently or assume I was unfit if they knew. As time went on, I realized that hiding this part of my identity was making it more difficult for me to come to work because I couldn't be myself or ask for help when I needed it. The associated stress was making my condition worse. When I interviewed at Gravity, I made a conscious decision to be upfront about my mental illness, especially since I was applying to lead TA and knew I had an opportunity to bring awareness to an issue that confronts a huge portion of the workforce.

During the interview, Dan asked me what the term "sacrifice" meant to me. I told him how I had recently decided to sacrifice my time and my privacy in order to create a podcast called *Silent Superheroes* about mental health at work. It was a huge moment for me—opening myself up to a stranger during a job interview—but I knew I had made the right decision when I was offered the job. In my welcome email to the company, I spoke openly about my bipolar disorder and have since made it a huge part of my mission here at the company to promote mental health at work.

How We Promote Diversity

1. Recruitment and Hiring: Our recruitment process is the first touchpoint a potential employee has with our company. It is also how we find each and every one of the talented, passionate individuals who make Gravity successful. By making diversity a priority in our recruitment and hiring process and paying attention to any practices that may inadvertently limit the talent pool, we make it easier to identify and attract candidates from a wide range of backgrounds. For example, our recruiters and hiring managers attend events and job fairs that cater to professionals from diverse backgrounds (e.g. Women in Technology, Lesbians Who Tech, the Orion Veteran Hiring Conference etc.). We have also designed objective hiring criteria that help us avoid unconscious bias (such as the use of scorecards that focus on skills, knowledge, achievements, and other relevant information) and improved our online application by allowing job-seekers to share their preferred gender pronouns. In addition, we sponsor h1B visas for candidates from foreign countries. These are just a few examples of how we strive to create a diverse workforce, and we welcome any and all suggestions for how we can continue to improve this process.

2. DIG: DIG (Diversity and Inclusion at Gravity) is an open group that started in 2015 after Nelson Pfab's announcement of their preferred pronouns spurred conversations about how the company could be more inclusive. DIG's guiding statement declares that its mission is to foster "an inclusive and diverse workplace" and "to actively engage in identifying diversity-related needs within the company and assist in addressing those needs." The DIG team identifies trainings, events, blog series, or recruitment opportunities, or other initiatives to help drive diversity and inclusion at the company. The group also sponsors speakers to come to our offices and discuss issues related to diversity in the wider community, like transgender rights and representation of people of color in the film industry. DIG is open to anyone at the company.

3. Onboarding: As part of the standard new-hire training, new employees at Gravity attend an orientation on DIG that introduces the group's mission, outlines current and previous diversity initiatives, and highlights the company's commitment to diversity in all its forms. In this way, new hires learn that diversity and inclusion are priorities on par with our three core values, company mission, and other policies and procedures.

4. Formal Policies and Procedures: Our employee Bill of Rights ensures that all employees "be treated with respect and dignity" by all other employees. Meanwhile, our Employee Handbook outlines a "Commitment to Inclusivity," which holds that "we all must hold each other accountable for providing a safe environment for every individual on the team to thrive" and that discrimination based on "age, culture, disabilities, ethnic origin, sex, parental status including pregnancy, gender identity and/or expression, marital, civil union or domestic partnership status, nationality, race, religion, sexual orientation, political ideology or party affiliation, and veteran and socioeconomic status, or any other status protected by the laws or regulations in the locations where we have employees or merchants" will not be tolerated. These documents not only indicate the type of culture we strive to promote but also empower employees and managers to address and correct any instance of intolerance knowing they have the full support of the company behind them.

5. Customer and Employee Touchpoints: Even small interactions with those we serve—both inside and outside the company—can go a long way in fostering diversity and inclusion. Some of the ways we do this are by providing gender-neutral restrooms and preferred-pronoun buttons at our Seattle office. We also encourage people to include their preferred pronouns in their email signatures if they are comfortable doing so.

6. Diversity-Themed Blog Posts: For the past few years, we have featured several series on our blog[5] that profile employees from various diverse backgrounds. In the past, we've done a series on diversity, women in leadership, faith and values, and veterans. Even when we publish a profile that isn't explicitly related to diversity, we seek to highlight the diverse backgrounds and perspectives each and every one of our team members brings to the organization.

7. Seeking Feedback from Those with Alternate Perspectives: One of the best ways to ensure diversity of thought is to seek feedback directly from those who have a different background or with whom you tend to disagree. For example, while

---

[5] See: www.gravitypayments.com/highlights/

Dan Price has been an outspoken advocate of left-leaning/progressive business policies, he often seeks feedback on ideas and initiatives from team members who lean to the right on those issues. Brooke Carey, Lead Storyteller, also frequently seeks feedback on pieces of writing that touch on diverse topics.

We Can Always Do Better

We've come a long way in our commitment to diversity, but we recognize that we can always do better. Our Passion for Progress requires us to constantly seek ways to grow and improve, so we value any and all suggestions from anyone at the company about how we can improve diversity at Gravity.

Questions for Reflection

1. In your opinion, what makes a company inclusive? What is something we as a company could do to improve our culture of inclusivity? What needs to happen for us to be successful at it? Who can you share your idea with?

   _____
   _____
   _____

2. When we talk about diversity and inclusion, are there elements you don't understand or agree with? Have you spoken to someone—a Team Advocate, DIG representative, or another co-worker—to gain clarity? If so, how did the conversation go? If not, consider starting a dialogue.

   _____
   _____
   _____

3. What are some areas for improvement when it comes to diversity and inclusion? How would you propose addressing these areas? Who can you talk to about these ideas?

   _____
   _____
   _____

PART III
RESPONSIBILITY

In 2016, a major industry update known as SHA-2 or "SHApocalypse" or as it was known throughout Gravity—required that every single terminal in the field be manually updated to help provide additional security. To prepare for the early December deadline, the Deployment Team had worked for months to finish the job, but come November, they still had about 800 terminals left to update. With just a few weeks to go before the SHApocalypse hit, all remote Deployment reps flew into Seattle for an all-hands-on-deck week of work. While the Seattle team continued to manage the regular caseload, the remote reps worked to finish the update.

Updating each terminal required building the new software online, downloading the file to the new terminal, testing the new terminal using a different program on a computer, repackaging the box with the terminal, two ethernet cables, and a user manual, printing out the shipping label and attaching it to the right box, and, finally, shipping the terminal to the merchant. Despite working overtime, come Thursday, the team still had 300 terminals left to update, and they realized that, without some help, they'd never finish the job on time.

Jose Garcia, who managed Deployment at the time, reached out to the rest of the company to see if anyone would be free on Friday to help. Immediately, people began to volunteer, and soon, people from every department—from Finance to Marketing to Sales—started helping out. Dan Price came in to help stuff boxes and ship. Tammi Kroll stayed late to work with the team. Basically, the Deployment Department more than doubled in size that night and everyone formed a makeshift assembly line to help finish the job as quickly and efficiently as possible. So many people showed up to help that the team actually finished several hours earlier than expected—and ended up having a lot of fun in the process. "Because it was after hours, we could be loud, play music, and joke around, so while we were all working our butts off, we could still enjoy each other's company," recalls David Shaw, a Deployment

Rep from Oklahoma. "It was exhausting but exhilarating. If you reach out for help, there are always twenty people there ready and willing to help you, no questions asked. It's about sacrifice, and how everyone at Gravity is willing to sacrifice their time and energy in order to accomplish something to help their team."

David's sentiment encapsulates our third core value of Responsibility. Responsibility can seem like a stodgy word—evoking thoughts of chores or budgeting or other necessary but boring tasks. ==Our definition of Responsibility transcends this traditional connotation and is meant to inspire a deep feeling of ownership, pride, community, respect, and dignity among everyone who works with and for Gravity Payments.== When we embrace our core value of Responsibility, we naturally take ownership of ourselves, our teams, and our company, which helps us feel connected to our common purpose and allows us to work together toward our shared vision. We take Responsibility for ourselves by behaving with integrity. We take Responsibility for one another by practicing empathy. And we take Responsibility for the organization through teamwork.

CHAPTER 7
INTEGRITY

The credit card processing and merchant services industry is notorious for engaging in bad behavior. At best, many of our competitors charge unnecessarily high fees in exchange for shoddy customer service that makes merchants less able to run their businesses efficiently. At worst, we've seen evidence of payment processors charging hidden fees, raising rates without giving their clients advance notice, or even outrightly lying to merchants in an attempt to secure their business and/or extract more money from them.

Knowing this, we could easily gain a competitive advantage by simply charging lower rates and offering decent customer service. But our value of Responsibility requires us to do more than simply be less awful than other providers out there. It requires us to take ownership of the success and well-being of those we serve and act accordingly.

As such, we strive to act with integrity in everything we do—especially when it comes to our merchants and even if it means we lose money in the short term. For example, if we learn we cannot beat another processor's rates, or if we know we cannot provide the proper payment or software solution for a merchant or partner, we will say so and explain why. Sometimes, this works to our advantage as a business owner might appreciate our honesty and decide to work with us even if we will charge them more. Other times, we simply lose their business. To us, the outcome is not what matters, but rather the fact that we know we did what was best for the client and not ourselves.

Jon Lien, Accountant, Seattle
The Working Capital Team works with merchants who are looking for a quick infusion of cash to help fund their businesses, but we only work with merchants who have already signed with us. So, a lot of times, I'll get a call from someone who has heard about our capital program and wants to know if we'll cover their balance from another processor if they sign with us. We can do this pretty easily, but what the merchants typically don't think about is that they'll just be transferring their debt somewhere else and, because we have to charge them a fee for the service, they'll end up paying a second fee on the money they've already received without really getting much benefit. That's because the money we'll be offering them goes directly to paying off the other company, but their overall balance will end up increasing. I know that a lot of merchants don't think about the logistics of this, but I'm always upfront with them about the reality, and, in many cases, that means they don't sign with us—at least not right away. I have had merchants come back to us later and say they want to sign with us because they appreciated how transparent we were with them. But if they don't come back, then at least I know we did the right thing.

I've also recently been getting calls from a lot of business owners who want know why we can't approve them for as much money as one of our biggest competitors. What they don't realize is that our competitor only looks at the merchant's processing volume, but we also look at their bank accounts to make sure they have enough liquidity to afford the expected monthly payments. The other company may approve the merchant for $35,000 when we can only approve them for $20,000, but a larger advance usually means larger monthly payments. We make sure to only offer terms that will allow the merchant a bit of wiggle room in their account even while making payments—something that the other company doesn't factor in at all when trying to win their business. I tell them that, as annoying as it is to have to provide us bank statements, and as much as they may want more money upfront, we're trying to consider what's best for their business in the long-term. That means we're not going to approve them for a loan that will be a burden for them to repay.

Sometimes being transparent means we lose business, but I don't consider it my duty to drum up as much business as possible. I consider it my duty to give our merchants the tools they need to make the right decisions, and that means being honest about what's best for the future of their business.

Integrity also requires that we admit when we are wrong and take action to rectify our mistakes. Did we set up an account incorrectly so a merchant was charged more than they owed? We will pay them back. If a vendor or third party makes a mistake that ends up costing a merchant, we may decide to refund the merchant the money directly, even if we did not cause the error. Likewise, if we notice an error on an account, we will notify the merchant and rectify the problem immediately--even if the merchant was unaware there was a problem in the first place.

But ==integrity, for us, goes beyond doing the right thing when it's evident what the right thing is. Integrity also requires us to do everything within our power to fulfill our mission of helping the little gal or guy.== This means going beyond what is simply right and what is expected to deliver an experience our merchants will not get anywhere else. It means driving two hours out of our way to have a face-to-face meeting to rectify a problem or to deliver hardware that a merchant needs right away. It means floating a partner cash so they can continue to operate while a major account error is rectified. It means dedicating as much time to fix a problem for a client who processes $10,000 a month as we would for a client who processes $100,000 a month. It means making ten extra phone calls to track down the source of a problem. It means adhering to our core values of Responsibility and Creative Leadership to come up with solutions that help our merchants no matter what.

Oscar Cauich, Engineer, Seattle
Edwin Dutton, who heads up our Finance Department, noticed that one of our merchants, a fine-dining restaurant in West Seattle, hadn't settled its account in several weeks. Apparently, a corrupted transaction had prevented their point-of-sale (POS) system from settling an entire batch of transactions, and the restaurant had about $80,000 in pending transactions whose authorization codes were about to expire. The Sales Rep in charge of the account tried reaching out to the owner to let him know what was going on, but he couldn't reach him, so he asked me if I could try to settle the batch on his behalf. I was somewhat familiar with this POS system, but not enough to figure out what was going on. So we called the POS company's support department directly. The person we spoke to said that, since the merchant didn't have a support contract with them, they had no way of remoting in to settle the batch. So we decided to go ahead and pay for the extra support on behalf of the merchant so the issue could be resolved.

To this day, I have no idea if the merchant ever knew what happened, but the story just goes to show how we're willing to do whatever we can to help our merchants succeed.

Emiley Stringfield, Sales, Boise
We work with several merchants in Texas who were hit hard by Hurricane Harvey in 2017. One of those merchants was an outdoor power-equipment company, and the owner needed some way to sell generators even though his internet and phone lines were knocked out by the storm. In order to be able to do business, he set up a PayPal account and ran transactions through it for several hours before his credit card terminal got back online. During that time, he processed more than $140,000 in revenue, but he didn't realize until afterward that PayPal's policy was to hold the money for thirty days. On top of that, PayPal's rates are way higher than ours, so this owner was, understandably, freaking out.

When he called to explain the situation to me, I felt horrible but didn't think there was anything I could do for him. I had no control over what PayPal did with their clients' money, so I told him how awful I felt but couldn't offer anything in the way of help. Later that day, I told a few people in the office about what had happened and Tammi's daughter Tausha, who worked here at the time, told me to expect a call from her mom. I couldn't imagine what Tammi could do to help, but she called me and told me she'd make a few calls and get back to me. Later that day, she forwarded an email to me from someone very high up at PayPal saying that the company would release the money to our partner right away, no problem. Turns out, this guy was an old friend of Tammi's, so she'd called him up and he'd done her a favor.

Obviously, not everyone can call up a VP at PayPal and get them to do what they want, and Tammi certainly didn't have to call in a personal favor for a partner who had processed with another company. But the fact that someone as busy as Tammi would take the time to go above and beyond for a client in this way speaks to the heart of what we're about as a company. If it's within our power to help a small business owner, we'll make it happen.

Integrity also applies to our internal relationships and allows us to live out our core value of Responsibility in our interactions with our fellow team members. We strive to support one another in whatever way we can, even if it is inconvenient or disadvantageous for us to do so in the short term. As we do with our merchants and partners, we commit to doing what we promise we're going to do and admitting when we make mistakes. We are honest and open and will not lie to or deceive our colleagues in order to avoid a difficult conversation. Instead of simply pointing out or complaining about the mistakes of others, we help them address and rectify those mistakes. We reject gossip and office politics in favor of direct communication, and we seek to understand internal problems fully rather than make assumptions about the actions or motivations of others. This not only creates a more positive and productive work environment in which people feel free to focus on their jobs instead of worrying about interpersonal dynamics; it also creates a culture of growth and development that is in keeping with our value of Responsibility.

James Pratt, Vice President of People Development, Seattle
In late 2018, TA hired an external consultant to conduct a company-wide sexual harassment training. It had been a couple of years since we'd had a formal training like this and, in light of the #MeToo movement promoting increased awareness of sexual harassment in the workplace, we felt it was an appropriate time to have an internal discussion.

Unfortunately, the training fell short of many people's expectations and left several people angry, hurt, and upset by the way it was conducted. We received many comments from people who attended one of the two trainings offered, and while the specific grievances varied, the consensus was clear: we, as a company, had failed to provide a safe, inclusive environment in which to discuss an incredibly sensitive topic.

A few other members of TA and I met with DIG as well as a few other team members to discuss the training more candidly. Even though there were only a few people in the room, it was apparent that the damage had extended beyond the people who had chosen to speak up directly. The representatives from TA considered several ways in which we could respond and decided that, ultimately, the best thing to do was to apologize, accept responsibility for what had happened, and resolve to do better next time. We sent an email to the entire company disclosing some of the feedback and acknowledging the hurt the training had caused. It was a humbling moment for someone like me who prides himself on making the workplace better for all employees. But, ultimately, my integrity as a person and our integrity as a team and as a company required us to fix the mistake we had made.

Questions for Reflection

1. How do you regularly practice integrity in your job? How do you feel when you behave with integrity?

   _____
   _____
   _____

2. Think of a time when you did something that turned out badly for someone else. How did you respond? If you could do it again, what would you do differently?

   _____
   _____
   _____

3. Think of the last time you made a mistake that involved someone else. How did you respond once you found out? How did you feel? What did you do to rectify it?

   _____
   _____
   _____

CHAPTER 8
EMPATHY

We define empathy as the ability to understand, appreciate, and relate to the feelings of others by putting yourself in their shoes. Empathy is different from sympathy or compassion because it requires taking the time to consider how and why another person might be feeling the way they do even—and especially—when those feelings are seemingly in direct conflict with our own.

==Practicing empathy requires us to do something that is simple but not always easy: remember that each and every person with whom we interact is a human being whose feelings are just as valid as our own.== Too often, when moving through our day-to-day lives and trying to accomplish everything on our to-do lists, we forget this basic truth and treat others as either roadblocks or stepping stones to our success, rather than human beings with their own unique passions, goals, emotions, beliefs, and challenges. If we see someone as a roadblock, we, at best, ignore them and, at worst, treat them with disdain or even outright contempt. If we view them as stepping stones, we may behave politely or helpfully toward them, but we do so only to the extent that we think it will help us get what we want. This is not empathy but opportunism, and it creates superficial, quid pro quo relationships.

This is especially true at work. We suck up to those who can help us advance in our careers—clients, managers, and those in positions of influence—while we ignore or demean those we don't view as valuable—like an assistant or junior person in another department or the person who delivers our mail.

But behaving without empathy is not only selfish, it's counterproductive. ==When we take the time to consider another person's feelings and circumstances—to empathize with them—we open the door to better communication, understanding, and trust, which in turn allows for better problem solving and improved relationships.== Practicing empathy involves taking the time to ask questions such as, "What can I provide this person? How can I help? What does this person need?" rather than, "What can I get from this person? How can this person help me?"

Empathy requires us to look at our merchants, not as revenue sources or metrics, but as business owners who are trying to provide for their employees, customers, communities, and families—just like we are. It requires us to remember that the reason they want to work with us is because we can help them fulfill this mission by providing low rates and superior service. When we remember this motivation, we can open a dialogue that puts it—as opposed to our desire to close a sale—at the center. When we do this, we naturally put ourselves in a position to serve our merchants, and, in turn, our merchants will be able to tell that we are on their side. Once you see someone as a human being, it becomes almost impossible to disrespect or lie to them.

We must also treat our fellow team members with empathy by remembering that we are all in this together and all of us are trying to do our jobs the best way we know how. Even when someone is behaving in a way that we'd prefer they not—not responding to our emails as quickly as we like or making mistakes on work that we then have to fix—rarely is it because they have bad intentions. When problems arise, empathy allows us to assume that everyone involved is acting out of good intentions, which, in turn, allows us to have productive conversations and come up with effective, win-win solutions.

Yuri Prater, IT Specialist, Seattle
Like they do with everyone who starts at the company, TA asked me to write a short paragraph to include in the email they sent to the team on my first day. Rather than just talk about where I was from or my previous work experience, I decided to have a little fun by mentioning my love of things like comic books and 90s music and throwing in a few pop-culture references that I figured might amuse a few people if they bothered to read the message. I was not expecting anyone to really put much effort into reading the email; Maybe a couple glances or a skim before it got moved to the delete folder, but nothing super detailed.

So I was surprised when, within my first few days at the company, people from various departments referenced several of the things I had mentioned directly to me. For example, a few people wanted to debate me on how I ranked each of the *Star Wars* movies (57834612, for the record), or asked if I had seen *Solo: A Star Wars Story* (which had just been released). Another agreed with me that the infamous dress was, in fact, white and gold (something I forgot I put in the email!) The one exchange that really sold me on Gravity's environment and people involved my opinion on the ending of *Titanic*. I said there was enough room on the door for Jack, and one of our Deployment Reps Slacked me a Facebook comment (with mathematical equations) proving that while there was enough room for Jack on the door, the extra weight would have caused it to sink, killing him and Rose.

It feels really welcoming when people aren't just saying hi because you're new but are actually taking an interest in who you are and what you say by talking to you about the things you enjoy. To actually have people comment on and joke about things I shared and make me feel welcome by using them as an opportunity to connect with me—that's not something I've witnessed at any other place I've worked.

We should strive to act with empathy in every interaction we have, no matter how routine. When requesting information or action from someone else—whether you're a Sales Rep opening a high-priority case for Deployment, a new employee asking for feedback from your manager, or a team member asking for help from IT—you can do so empathetically by taking the time to explain the situation completely, asking politely, and—as obvious as it sounds—saying, "thank you." Being pleasant and civil in your communication requires a little extra thought, but it doesn't require any extra time, and it can go a long way toward demonstrating to the other person that you respect them.

Another way to practice empathy is to consider what someone else needs instead of focusing solely on what you're trying to get out of a situation. This is especially helpful if the other person is angry or upset. Oftentimes, the first thing a person needs when they're upset is for someone else to validate their feelings. Simply saying, "I understand that you are upset" can go a long way in diffusing a tense situation and opening the door to a more productive conversation because it signals to the other person that you're listening. Another way to validate someone is to repeat back to them the things they tell you so you can be sure you understand them. These simple gestures not only help to de-escalate tense situations, but they also make it easier for both parties to empathize with one another and work together to find resolution.

A Culture of Empathy

Civility, while important, is not the same as empathy. Many organizations practice civility in their communications and interactions but limit interpersonal relationships and conversations to what goes on at the office while discouraging talk about one's personal life. But, again, the people with whom you work are not just co-workers or clients; they are human beings whose personal lives and circumstances influence their work in ways both obvious and invisible. If one of your team members is ill or dealing with a family emergency, those personal issues will most certainly interfere with their work life. Ignoring those issues discounts the humanity of that person and prevents you from identifying ways you can help. It also makes it more difficult for this person to come to work, as they feel they have to deal with these serious problems on their own and mask any sign of vulnerability at the risk of being deemed unprofessional, weak, or incompetent.

That's why we strive to create a safe, supportive space in which individuals can feel comfortable discussing both the ups and downs of their personal lives with their colleagues if they want to. Allowing people to share both the struggles and triumphs of their lives with one another promotes empathy by reminding those around you of your shared humanity. At the same time, it promotes a strong culture in which people feel responsible to those around them and are therefore willing to go above and beyond to help when necessary.

Although a culture of empathy can only grow through the actions of individual team members, we do strive to promote it through certain formal policies and procedures. For instance, TA is available to discuss any personal or professional issues that require attention. Whether it's a request for parental leave or a conversation about a personal issue that will temporarily affect your ability to work a normal schedule, they are here to help figure out a solution. At other organizations, human resources often acts as little more than an extension of the corporate legal team, doing what they must to coordinate benefits and protect the legal and financial interests of the company without considering the unique needs of each individual. TA, by contrast, strives to understand each employee's circumstances so they can propose solutions that will address their specific needs. While we hope people will feel comfortable sharing their lives at work, we also respect the need for privacy, so team members can request full confidentiality on sensitive conversations they have with their managers or anyone within TA. At the same time, we encourage managers to consistently check in with their direct reports in an effort to promote open communication.

We also promote empathy by providing our team members opportunities to form relationships and bond with one another and members of our community. Whether it's bringing the team together at our annual kickoff party each January, organizing a volunteer or donation event through our Gravity Gives program, inviting new hires out to a group dinner at one of our merchants, or simply encouraging impromptu interactions through our open-office floor plans, we encourage personal interactions outside of our day-to-day work knowing that it creates a stronger, mure humane environment in which everyone can thrive.

When we remember the humanity in others, we bring out the humanity in ourselves and, in so doing, create a culture of trust and responsibility in which we can all thrive.

Empathy in Action

Acting with empathy may seem obvious, but it can be difficult to do so when you're busy, distracted, or focused on a personal goal—like signing a new client, advancing your career, or even something as run-of-the-mill as getting information from a colleague. Below are simple things you can do to get in the habit of practicing empathy in everyday interactions.

- Greet the other person by name. If you don't know their name, ask.
- Give the other person your full attention. Look them in the eye if speaking face-to-face and don't multitask when they are speaking to you, whether it's over the phone, in a meeting, in a group, or one-on-one.
- Connect on something personal—a favorite sports team, a common hobby, a mutual friend, or something else.
- Relax and be yourself. While it's important to remain professional, people, especially strangers, tend to prefer talking to people with whom they can relate. Sharing a bit of your personality helps them empathize with you as well because it reminds them that you are a human being.
- Assume positive intent. As discussed in the section on feedback, when we assume that other people have good intentions, we automatically interpret their actions differently, which, in turn, changes our response. If you encounter rudeness or hostility, assume the person is simply having a bad day and you'll be less likely to take their words or behaviors personally.
- Listen to understand. Don't just wait until it's your turn to speak; pay attention to what the other person is saying and respond accordingly. If you don't understand something, ask questions to clarify their meaning.

Questions for Reflection

1. What are the main sources of interpersonal conflict in your role at the company? How can you practice empathy in those situations?

   _____
   _____
   _____

2. Consider a time when practicing empathy helped you resolve a conflict or reach a mutual goal with someone else. How did this experience make you feel? What did you do to empathize with that person? What did they do to empathize with you?

   _____
   _____
   _____

3. Think back to a situation in which a lack of empathy caused a problem to escalate or increased conflict between you and someone else. What could you have done differently to diffuse the tension and practice empathy in that situation?

   _____
   _____
   _____

CHAPTER 9
TEAMWORK

While we value autonomy and the right of every individual to be able to contribute to our company in the way they feel is best, we also recognize that people must be able to work together and support one another in order for an organization to thrive. When people are willing to come together and work as a team, they become more efficient and powerful. Collectively, they can use their individual talents and skills to generate and execute on ideas, tasks, and initiatives that move the company forward.

The Sales Team needs the Support, Finance, Marketing, and Development Teams to deliver on their promises in order to keep clients satisfied, while those teams rely on Sales to provide information and set expectations with our merchants and partners in order to do their jobs effectively. If, at any point, someone on one of these teams fails to cooperate, everyone suffers.

While each individual and department has a specific, assigned function and area of focus within the organization, we are all united around the common mission of helping independent businesses succeed. Each of us has a responsibility to do this in whatever way possible, even if that way falls outside our formal job descriptions. Responsibility requires us to put our egos aside and ask, "How can I help?" It means proactively offering to help someone whom we see struggling rather than waiting to be asked or assuming there's nothing we can do to assist. We all have the capacity to contribute to the organization beyond our job descriptions, just like the team members who helped with the SHA-2 update, described earlier, exemplified.

A task need not directly involve a merchant or partner in order to support our core mission. For example, something as mundane as running the communal dishwasher when you notice there are no clean dishes or helping set up or clean up after an in-office event frees up the coworkers who would otherwise have to deal with these things to focus on more important tasks.

Teamwork is not just about efficiency or productivity, however. It is also about creating the company you want to work for. When people feel supported by their co-workers, relationships between coworkers improve. Research has shown that one's interpersonal relationships at the office have a profound impact on how satisfied they are at work, and when people are satisfied at work, they are more likely to stay in their jobs for longer.[6] Higher retention not only helps save a company money, but it also increases productivity. In short, teamwork is good for you, your coworkers, and your company.

At Gravity, we promote a spirit of teamwork through several

---

[6] Jan-Emmanuel de Neve, "Work and Well-being: A Global Perspective," Global Happiness Policy Report 2018, p.86, http://www.happinesscouncil.org/report/2018/.

formal policies and procedures. Our open-office floor plans in the Seattle and Boise offices allow people from different departments to observe what is going on with one another and strike up conversations, which may reveal ways they might be able to help out. Open communication channels like Slack also allow for quick access to others at the company who may be able to help with a question or a problem. Organized Slack groups also provide regular opportunities for team members to help out their co-workers. For example, in the know-your-customer (#kyc-delivery) channel, team members can volunteer to drop off equipment or other resources to merchants in neighborhoods that might not be convenient for those directly in charge of the account. Likewise the private front desk channel allows participants to cover shifts at the front desk when necessary. Formal group activities like volunteer events organized by our Gravity Gives team and group outings, like sporting events, picnics, or karaoke nights, also promote teamwork by allowing people to get to know one another and have impromptu chats outside of the office.

But the main way in which we encourage teamwork is through demonstrating it on a daily basis in our interactions with one another. Every time a person asks for help and receives it or someone offers to pitch in without being asked, we demonstrate that we value one another and share a common goal.

> **Edwin Dutton, Vice President of Finance, Seattle**
> The Finance team gets a lot of proposals on any given day, and one of our team members, Cody Boorman, has earned a reputation for getting them done extremely quickly. During a discussion about his career, the topic of how he was able to get cases done so quickly came up, and he said the reason was twofold. First, he knew how much it helped out our Sales Team, and therefore also helped our merchants, to get them information on pricing quickly. That was pretty straightforward, but what I found most striking was the

second reason he gave. He said he had such a focus on turning around proposals quickly because the more work he was able to get done, the more time his teammates would have to work on other projects that they found more interesting or that could help improve the department in other ways. I was really impressed with this because clearly Cody was able to find a purpose in his day-to-day work that connects even simple things to a larger idea, plus he's also leading by example, serving others, and working in a spirit of teamwork to help drive everyone on the team and the company forward. This way of finding purpose and serving others is something I look up to and think we can always have more of.

Questions for Reflection

1. Are there parts of your job you could use help on? Who is in a position to help? Have you reached out to that person/group asking for assistance?

   _____
   _____
   _____

2. What are some ways in which you help your coworkers that are not included in your official job description? How do you feel when you help in this way? Are there other ways you could help?

   _____
   _____
   _____

PART IV
OUR COMPENSATION PHILOSOPHY

Dan Price got a lot of attention when he announced a new living wage at Gravity in April 2015. But the roots of our company's commitment to providing fair compensation are much deeper than the headlines revealed. Our compensation philosophy is informed directly by our core mission of helping business owners, and it helps us create the culture we want for our organization.

In deciding to enact a living wage, Dan realized that our team members could not adequately take care of our merchants if they could not adequately take care of themselves. This is not charity; it's common sense. If someone has to work a second job or commute three hours a day because they cannot afford to live closer to the office, they simply will not have the time, energy, or focus to give 100% to their work every day. At the same time, if a surprise expense like a car repair or hospital bill threatens to wipe out someone's savings, the stress of that situation could negatively impact their performance at work.

Whether or not they admit it, most companies treat money and profit as the sole reason for their existence. They measure their success by how much money they are making and treat expenses as enemies that need to be limited. Because payroll typically makes up an organization's primary expense, compensation is treated as a necessary evil and something to be limited whenever possible.

At Gravity we take a different view of money that allows us to approach compensation differently. Instead of looking at money as a sign of success or failure, we view it as a tool to help us achieve our goal of helping the little guy or gal business owner succeed. While we need a certain amount of money in order to stay in business and protect ourselves in the event of an emergency or market downturn, we don't consider profit to be all that important. Because we have let go of the need to increase profit as much as possible, we can use the money we do have to invest in our team, which we believe is the best strategy for serving our merchants. If we can hire more people and pay them a wage that not only allows them to get by but to thrive, we will be in a better position to meet our customers' needs and go above and beyond in our efforts to serve them.

Everyone Is Underpaid

While everyone at Gravity starts at a relatively high salary, we believe in helping each and every person increase that compensation as quickly as possible. This, too, marks a difference in how we view compensation compared to most other companies. At most companies, an employee's compensation is determined by their market value—essentially how much it would cost to replace them. This means that, simply by virtue of their job title, some employees are "worth" inherently more than others.

==Here, we determine how much to pay someone based on the value they bring to the company, not on their supposed market value.== This is a much trickier metric to determine because most of this value cannot be easily measured. Even in a metrics-heavy department like Sales, in which you can easily determine how much revenue an individual is bringing into the company, there is still no way to account for the intangible values a particular rep brings to their job. Perhaps a rep's merchants are loyal to them because they have consistently gone out of their way to offer exceptional service. Or perhaps they bring a unique communication style to their interactions that helps to build trust and empathy with potential clients. This might not be reflected in their numbers, but it is still extremely valuable to the company.

A person's value increases as they gain new skills and take on new responsibilities, which, as we outlined in the section on growth and development, is something we encourage all employees to do. As your value increases, so should your compensation. In fact, we want our people to be pursuing so many opportunities that, at any given time, they are actually underpaid because their value to the company is increasing at a faster rate than their salary.

Compensation Plans and Conversations

The first item on our Employee Bill of Rights states that each employee is entitled to "develop compensation goals and a career development plan" with their manager. We believe each and every employee is entitled to this conversation because we believe that helping our people achieve their financial goals makes us stronger as an organization.

In order to make sure your compensation continues to increase alongside your value, we help facilitate compensation conversations between employees and managers at regular intervals. All new employees should expect to have this conversation with their manager within the first three to six months of them starting at the company. Longer-term employees should plan to have a formal conversation with their manager ideally once every three months to ensure consistent accountability and allow for the plan to be changed if necessary. During these conversations, you are free to discuss compensation goals, both short and long term, with your manager and then work with your manager to figure out how you might be able to expand your role and responsibilities in order to attain that goal. Together, you and your manager can identify opportunities and priorities that will allow you to get to where you want to be.

Before having a compensation conversation with your manager, take the time to consider your actual compensation goals. Many people find this challenging, especially when thinking about where they want to be financially five, ten, or twenty years from now. While we encourage you to think as long-term as possible, breaking down your goals into smaller steps and considering specific life goals—as opposed to a certain number—can help you figure out where you want to be.

For example, when trying to arrive at a number, consider the following questions:

- **Are you in debt?**
  The average college graduate has over $30,000 in student loan debt, which means they are already behind financially before they start earning a steady income. Carrying debt of any kind will keep you from achieving your financial goals, so it's important to try and get out of debt as quickly as possible. When considering your compensation goals, calculate how much debt you're currently carrying—from student loans, credit cards, mortgages, car payments, or any other type—and how quickly you'd like to pay it off.

- **Are you/do you plan to get married?**
  Whether you choose to formally tie the knot or simply move in with your partner, joining forces with another person financially will ease some of your own income needs since you'll be able to share rent and other expenses. However, if you make more than your partner or if you end up having to support your partner financially for some reason, you'll need to make more than you would if you were on your own. While it's impossible to predict the future, having a sense of who else will be affected by your financial situation will help you figure out where you need to be.

- **Do you have/plan to have children?**
  The US government estimates that it costs $233,610 to raise one child—not including the cost of college.[7] Keep in mind, however, that this is an *average* cost, which means if you live in an expensive place (like Seattle or Hawaii) or if you plan on spending additional money to raise your children—by sending them to private school, for instance—that number will go up. Even if you are still years away from having children, if you want to start a family, you should

---

[7] Aimee Pichi, "Raising a child costs $233,610. Are you financially prepared to be a

consider the cost when plotting your financial goals.

- **Do you want to buy a home?**
  Buying property can be a great investment, but it's also an expensive one. Consider home prices where you live and what type of home you'd like to buy and where. How much would you need to save for a down payment? How much would your mortgage be? Most experts suggest that your mortgage (or rent) payment should not exceed 25 percent of your monthly take-home (aka net) pay, so your income will determine what type of home you can afford.

- **How much do you want to save for retirement?**
  Saving for retirement can seem like a far-off concern, especially if you are just starting out in your career. But the earlier you start saving, the better off you'll be when it comes time to retire. Many experts suggest saving between 10-15 percent of your annual gross income for retirement, and the higher your salary/lower your expenses are today, the more you can set aside for tomorrow.

- **What type of lifestyle do you want to lead?**
  Do you love to travel? Are you into adventure sports? Is life for you incomplete without a boat? Are you into fine wines or collectible art? Do you want to be able to donate large sums to charity or tithe to your house of worship? How much extra income would you need per year in order to live your ideal lifestyle?

In the aftermath of the $70k decision, we saw a quintupling in the number of team members who were able to start families as well as a 130 percent increase in 401(k) contributions. In addition, several team members were able to move to nicer homes closer to the office, thus reducing their commute times,

---

parent?" USA Today, February 26, 2018, https://www.usatoday.com/story/money/personalfinance/2018/02/26/raising-child-costs-233-610-you-financially-prepared-parent/357243002/.

a process that has been shown to increase happiness and reduce stress. All of these changes show how an increase in salary can dramatically improve one's life. What do those improvements look like to you?

Having a conversation about compensation at the same time you have a conversation about performance and career goals ensures that everyone is on the same page about where you hope to be both professionally and financially within a certain amount of time This not only benefits you by ensuring you have transparency into how you are being compensated, it also benefits the company because research has shown that clear communication around compensation encourages employee retention.

If you have not heard from your manager about having a compensation conversation, reach out to him or her now and ask to have one.

For more information on planning your financial future, check out the resources in Appendix A of this book.

IN CLOSING

As you move through your career at Gravity, we hope you will embrace the values and ideas in this book. We also hope you will refer to this book when making decisions, solving problems, resolving conflict, planning for the future, communicating with coworkers, and generally figuring out how to be successful.

That said, a book can never fully capture the intricacies of an organization or its culture. While this book is meant to be a guide to our culture, it does not pretend to be the last word on the subject. Organizations do not create culture; the people within them create culture. That's what we mean when we talk about Creators versus Consumers. If you see us failing to live up to our culture and values, or if you think the culture described in this book is no longer functioning the way it should, speak up.

In the meantime, if you have any questions about our culture, values, mission, or anything described in this book, please reach out to your manager or a member of TA to discuss.

APPENDIX A

For more information on the ideas described in this book, as well as many other topics related to culture and career development, check out the following resources.

Gravity's Learning and Development University

You can access the full library of past LDU sessions on Litmos. Sessions most relevant to our company values include "Giving Feedback" led by Bobby Powers, "Receiving Feedback" led by James Pratt and Bobby Powers, "Be Your Own CEO" led by Jen Peck, "Leading without a Title" led by Kaitlynn Vincent and Marcus Modugno, "Managing a Team" led by Rosita Barlow, and "Life from a Merchant's Perspective" led by Christy McDanold of Secret Garden Books.

Books

You'll find copies of many of the following books in the Seattle and Boise office libraries. You can also request books for the library by contacting Bobby Powers, Head of Learning and Development.

Highly Recommended for Everyone

Equip: The Gravity Leadership Playbook by Bobby Powers

The 7 Habits of Highly Effective People by Stephen R. Covey

Daring Greatly by Brené Brown

Death by Meeting by Patrick Lencioni

Drive by Daniel Pink

Getting to Yes by Roger Fisher, William Ury, and Bruce Patton

Good to Great by Jim Collins

Leaders Eat Last by Simon Sinek

The Power of Full Engagement by Jim Loehr and Tony Schwartz

Scaling Up (previously published as *Mastering the Rockefeller Habits*) by Verne Harnish

Switch by Chip and Dan Heath

Quiet by Susan Cain

General Business Acumen

Better Than Before by Gretchen Rubin

Blink by Malcolm Gladwell

Built to Last by Jim Collins

David and Goliath by Malcolm Gladwell

The E-Myth Revisited by Michael Gerber

Great by Choice by Jim Collins

Outliers by Malcolm Gladwell

The Power of Habit by Charles Duhigg

The Tipping Point by Malcolm Gladwell

Leadership/Management

The Checklist Manifesto by Atul Gawande

Dare to Lead by Brené Brown

The Five Dysfunctions of a Team by Patrick Lencioni

The Five Temptations of a CEO by Patrick Lencioni

Leadership and Self-Deception by The Arbinger Institute

Navigating The Growth Curve by James Fisher

The Speed of Trust by Stephen M. R. Covey

Tribal Leadership by Dave Logan, John King, and Halee Fischer-Wright

Self Improvement

The Art of Happiness by His Holiness the Dalai Lama

Decisive by Chip and Dan Heath

Ego is the Enemy by Ryan Holiday

Grit by Angela Duckworth

The Happiness Advantage by Shawn Achor

Mindset by Carol Dweck

Mountains Beyond Mountains by Tracy Kidder

The Obstacle is the Way by Ryan Holiday

Thanks for the Feedback by Douglas Stone and Sheila Heen

What Got You Here Won't Get You There by Marshall Goldsmith

Direct Communication

Crucial Conversations by Kerry Patterson, Joseph Grenny, Al Switzler, and Ron McMillan

Difficult Conversations by Douglas Stone and Sheila Heen

Radical Candor by Kim Scott

Sales and Sales Management

Let's Get Real or Let's Not Play by Mahan Khalsa and Randy Illig

The New Science of Selling and Persuasion by William Brooks

To Sell is Human by Daniel Pink

Spin Selling by Neil Rackham

Customer Service

Make It So by W Roberts and B Ross

Raving Fans by Ken Blanchard

Setting The Table by Danny Meyer

Finance

The Big Short by Michael Lewis

The Black Swan by Nassim Nicholas Taleb

Fooled by Randomness by Nassim Nicholas Taleb

Personal Finance

Clocking Out Early by Cody and Georgi Boorman

Financial Freedom by Grant Sabatier

How to Be Richer, Smarter, and Better Looking than Your Parents by Zac Bissonnette

I Will Teach You to Be Rich by Ramit Sethi

Smart Women Love Money by Alice Finn

Your Money or Your Life by Vicki Robin

Podcasts

General Business Acumen

How I Built This hosted by Guy Raz

WorkLife hosted by Adam Grant

Mental Health

Silent Superheroes hosted by James Pratt

TED Talks

General Business Acumen

"The Power of Introverts" by Susan Cain

Leadership/Management

"The Best Teams Have This Secret Weapon" by Adam Grant

"The Power of Vulnerability" by Brené Brown

"The Puzzle of Motivation" by Dan Pink

"Why Good Leaders Make You Feel Safe" by Simon Sinek

Made in the USA
Columbia, SC
04 March 2022